COMPLETE
SPECIAL EDUCATION
HANDBOOK

COMPLETE
SPECIAL EDUCATION
HANDBOOK

Katherine Geren

PARKER PUBLISHING COMPANY, INC.
WEST NYACK, NEW YORK

Library of Congress Cataloging in Publication Data

Geren, Katherine
    Complete special education handbook.

    Includes index.
    1.   Handicapped children--Education--Handbooks,
manuals, etc. I. Title.
LC4015.G397   371.9   79-15975
ISBN 0-13-164566-8

Printed in the United States of America

THE SCOPE AND PRACTICAL VALUE
THIS BOOK OFFERS

Written expressly for educators concerned with special education, this book will provide practical solutions to the problems which are thick in the special education field today. For example:

1. What *constitutes* an appropriate education for the handicapped?
2. How can the administrator be *sure* he's safeguarding the rights of children and parents?
3. Where can financial help be secured for expensive special education programs and related services?
4. What's the *real* meaning of "least restrictive environment"?
5. How do you go about implementing an IEP from start to finish?

Realistic, tested guidelines and programs are provided in this book. Readers who follow these ideas and suggestions will be able to improve existing programs and successfully initiate new ones, with the assurance that they are operating in compliance with PL 94-142.

It is said the success of a special education program can be attributed in large measure to the competence of the administrator. But competence can't operate with yesterday's information. It needs reliable, accurate input. And that is what this book is about. It provides up-to-date information and guidelines on specific ways to become a successful special education administrator. A number of illustrations will underscore the need for this book. ...

Recently, a parent brought her mentally retarded child to the neighborhood school for enrollment. After the administrator had observed the child, he told the mother the boy "wasn't ready," and recommended she keep him home for another year. The child lacked a month of being seven years old at the time. Amazingly, the person in charge wasn't fully aware of the law mandating a free appropriate education for all children of school age *regardless* of handicapping conditions. Later in the year, a third party informed the parent of her child's legal right to an education. Should a court case result from this incident (which is likely), the administrator might well wish he had spent some time carefully reviewing the guidelines in this handbook. He would have discovered all he needs to know about how to provide an "appropriate education" for the child.

Two other incidents, already in litigation, also occurred because of ignorance of the law:

...A school psychologist administered an individual psychological test to a child suspected of being mentally retarded, without first obtaining permission from the parent.

...A school district is being sued because it failed to make a sufficient effort to educate its handicapped children in the "least restrictive environment."

These unfortunate occurrences illustrate the costly path of learning by mistakes — something the user of this handbook will avoid. Each chapter is packed with information pertaining to special education administration, and wherever laws and legal regulations apply it is so noted.

But more than just presenting legal responsibilities, we will offer a wealth of "how-to-do-its." An underlying premise is that it's not enough to say *what* must be done. Specific directions, examples, and detailed suggestions for *ways to implement programs* are included with each topical presentation. In brief, the user of this handbook will have instant access to essential information on how to:

- Meet the challenge of Public Law 94-142 and its regulations
- Utilize key factors in the development of an efficient staff
- Design effective special education programs
- Work successfully in fulfilling regular education needs
- Prepare for productive meetings with staff, superintendent, and school board
- Interact positively and successfully with parents
- Speak with authority about the needs of handicapped students.
- Understand the financial aspects of special education on the federal, state, and local levels.

Nor is the psychology of administering a successful program overlooked. On occasion, the administrator needs more than a factual backlog of information. He can find himself in a position where he must demonstrate competence in the philosophical and psychological aspects of special education. The book presents numerous instances where these two factors become important. One example is the case of an administrator of special education whose office was the scene of this action:

> Within an hour after his return to work from the summer vacation, a dozen parents walked into this administrator's office and announced that they were entering children with problems ranging from mongolism to other severe types of handicaps, in the district schools. These parents were tense, determined, and informed. They had waited a long time to make this aggressive move, and it was apparent that they were not going to tolerate any interference or extended delay in carrying out their plan. An administrator in this position needs a tremendous amount of background information as well as feeling for the emotions of those involved. He has to grasp immediately the fact that this unannounced meeting may well be the most important business of the day — or perhaps the entire school term. A mishandling of the incident could set his program back months, if not years. The reaction of the news media, should they become interested in the story, the legal activity involved, school district policy — all this and more passes through his mind as he listens to what the parents are telling him. He makes careful mental notes and answers questions as they arise. And all the time he is thinking ahead. How much can he promise these parents? How can his schools handle the immediate enrollment of these seriously handicapped children who are coming from private schools, state institutions, and in some cases from the singularly protective environment of their own homes? What added staff might be needed? What educational diagnosis will be necessary for the children? What medical diagnosis, if any? But above all, he has to communicate with these parents confidently and accurately. And right *now.* Not promising more than his district can deliver, nor holding back on the district's responsibilities to *all* school age children.

This incident dramatically illustrates the need for the kind of aid this handbook offers. The administrator who has absorbed the essence and factual knowledge contained in the book won't find himself at a loss, even in a difficult situation such as the one described above. He'll be informed and will have examples of how to communicate this information. After reading this book, you will feel confident in using it as your guide to special education under PL 94-142. You will be tuned in to the distinctive ambience of special education, and at the same time you will comprehend its place in the total educational pattern. You will have what you need to become an outstanding administrator of special education in every sense of the word.

Katherine Geren

Contents

**How Changes Required by PL 94-142 Are Applied
to the Classroom** *(Continued)*

room Help During a Time of Change • How to React to Roadblocks • When to Employ a Holding Pattern • Summary

Characteristics of Good Teachers for All Children • Special
Classroom Requirements for the Handicapped • Six Ways You
Can Help Improve Classroom Instruction • How to Help with
Children Who Have Behavior Problems • Six Ways for Teachers
to Achieve and Maintain Outstanding Success • Administrative Factors That Influence Classroom Teaching • Key Factors
in Developing a Mainstreaming Package • Summary

What Is an Individualized Education Program? • Four Steps in
the Development of an IEP • Parents and the IEP • Format for
an IEP • Tips on Getting Parental Consent

What Hampers Parents from Becoming Involved? • Listen to
Parents, Don't Just Hear Them • How to Tell Parents About
Their Rights • Guidelines You Can Share with Parents • When
Parents Ask for an Evaluation of Their Child • Helping Parents
Understand the IEP • Six Steps That Foster Good Relationships
with Parents • Summary

How to Attack the Goal of Full Education for the Handicapped,
Ages 3-21 • Planning for Pre- and Post-School Age Children
• Tips on Alternate Ways to Serve Handicapped Children
• Key Factors in Contracting Services from Other Agencies
• Key Points in Handling Precedural Safeguards • Summary

Trouble Spots in the Laws • Watch Out for the Procedural Safe-
guards • Remember Parents' Rights • Try Mediation Instead of
Litigation • Don't Act Hastily—But Act • Be Careful About
What You Say and Write • Tips on Administering Medication to
Students • Be Prepared to Respond to Disruption • Liability
and Teachers' Rights • Here Are Some Extra "Do's" So You
Won't Be Sued • Summary

How to Be Monitored Successfully • Parents and Monitoring
• Hints on the Mechanics of Monitoring • Tips on Making
Facilities Safe for Children • Key Factors for Running a Better
Transportation Program • How to Serve Private School Chil-
dren Under PL 94-142 • Tips on Earning a Reputation for
Being Resourceful • Summary

COMPLETE SPECIAL EDUCATION HANDBOOK

Chapter One

Essential Facts
in the Administration of
Special Education

Don't avoid necessary decisions in the early months. Your previous judgments were good or you wouldn't have been promoted.

"Handicapped Law Passed!" "New Age Dawns for the Disabled." "Every Handicapped Child to Receive an Education — Millions Appropriated." Yesterday's newspapers were lavish with coverage of Public Law 94-142. Today the fanfare is over and you're into the long, hard pull of seeing that every handicapped child in your district is given an appropriate education in the least restrictive environment. The inequities of the past are ended as far as legislation is concerned. What we're faced with from now on is implementation.

Yesterday and Today in Special Education

The time is past when handicapped students were housed, taught, and over protected, far from the main current of the regular school operation. Special education isn't so "different" now. Its pattern is being woven into the main design of American education rather than forming the somber fringe areas of the past.

The responsibilities of the administrator of special education used to be relatively simple and clearcut:

1. Locate classroom building space.
2. Hire certified teachers.
3. Provide materials and equipment.
4. See that special classes have their full load: 100 speech cases for the speech therapist, 15 educable mentally retarded for the elementary room, 18 for the high school room, and so on.

Public Law 94-142 presents a different set of problems for the special education administrator, as these examples point out:

1. Is my district prepared for due process procedures?
2. What should I do about a consortium?
3. How can we make better use of the child census information mandated by PL 94-142?
4. Are we bringing all the children we can into regular classrooms?
5. Special transportation is beginning to cost as much as special instruction; what can be done about this?
6. The state educational agency has notified me of a monitoring visit to our district next month; I'm worried that our individual education programs (IEPs) may not be satisfactory.

The differences are obvious. Yet, we can't forget the old as we usher in the new. A postulate of this book is that we take what the old has taught, and apply it to achieve the newer, better goals. Many references are made concerning the value to the administrator in considering his or her district's traditional operations as he or she moves along with the implementation of PL 94-142.

Another postulate is that the job of providing handicapped children with an appropriate education cannot be done hurriedly. PL 94-142 was signed into perpetuity. It won't phase out. The final implementation was set for October 1, 1982 when funds, equaling 40 percent of the national average per pupil expenditure, are permanently authorized for the education of handicapped children.

To commence the implementation tasks let's start where the rules and regulations for PL 94-142 start — with definitions.

Identifying the "Special" Part of Special Education

The term "special education" means specially designed instruction, at no cost to the parent, to meet the unique needs of a handicapped child. ("At no cost" does not preclude incidental fees which are normally part of the regular education program.) Special education includes classroom instruction, instruction in physical education, home instruction, and instruction in hospitals and institutions. It includes speech pathology, vocational training, and any other service which meets the unique educational needs of the handicapped and is considered "special education" under your state standards.

Who are the handicapped children? The term "handicapped children" means those children, evaluated in accordance with Public Law 94-142 as being mentally retarded, hard of hearing, deaf, speech impaired, visually handicapped, seriously emotionally disturbed, orthopedically impaired, other health impaired, deaf-blind, multihandicapped, or as having specific learning disabilities, who because of those impairments need special education and related services. This last statement mentions the two major components of your program: "special education" and "related services." Let's clarify their meaning.

The Difference Between "Special Education" and "Related Services"

There's room for confusion here, but we can clear it up by examining federal and state standards. In PL 94-142 the services under "special education" all deal with specially designed instruction; they shouldn't be confused with "related services." Federal regulations define "related services" as special transportation, and such developmental, corrective, and other supportive services as are required to assist a handicapped child to benefit from special education. Related services include psychological services, physical and occupational therapy, recreation, early identification and assessment of disabilities in children, counseling services, and medical services for diagnostic or evaluation purposes. The term also includes health services, social work services in schools, parent counseling and training, and speech pathology and audiology. But — and here is the confusing part — speech pathology and other "related services" may also be considered "special education" if they consist of specially designed instruction. An example of this confusion might be in the area of speech pathology (speech therapy).

In your state, if speech pathology consists of specially designed instruction to meet the unique needs of the child, and if the service is considered special education under state standards, then the federal regulations will accept this service as special education. On the other hand, if a state considers speech pathology as a related service, the federal government will accept this category also. Because states differ in their classification of speech therapy, it was necessary to allow it to be defined under both special education and related services. This provision is not limited to speech pathology. It can be employed for any specially designed instructional service that your state standards consider special education, even though federal regulations list the activity as a related service.

Take the case of recreation for the handicapped. The federal definition lists recreation under related services. But if your state standards accept recreation as an instructional service, and a specially designed program is needed for handicapped children to benefit from this instruction, then your district can classify recreation as special education. Transportation and medical and diagnostic services cannot be placed in the special education category because by their very nature they do not provide specially designed instruction. These last three words, *specially designed instruction,* pinpoint the difference between special education and related services. Special education means special instruction.

Are you wondering why the emphasis on the distinction between the two terms? The point is that it is better to place all those services you can in the "special education" category rather than in the "related service" group, because it is the children served in special education who generate funds under PL 94-142. Children who receive *only* related services do not generate funds under PL 94-142. A specific case:

> A cerebral palsy child is able to get along without special education but needs special transportation to get to school. Federal funds under PL 94-142 will not assist in paying for this transportation since the child is not also receiving any specially designed instruction. Later on, if the child qualifies to receive special

education, perhaps in his high school physical education program, the district can claim financial assistance for his special transportation because he is now in special education.

Remember, we are talking about federal funding only. Your state educational agency (SEA) may reimburse local districts for related services whether or not the students are also receiving specially designed instruction. This is a distinction for the special education administrator to keep in mind when figuring his program costs, and when applying for federal funds.

Key Differences Between Your Program and Regular Education

We have defined special education and related services. Now we'll focus in on how these programs differ from regular education. A list of operations that take place in your program, over and above those required in the regular school system, will give you an idea of what your job consists of. You can use this list to line up your essential responsibilities, and as a frame of reference for your place in the education scene in your district. A special education program does the following:

1. Provides for an appropriate education for all handicapped children.
2. Operates under extensive federal laws, as well as under state statutes and local policies that apply to the education of handicapped children.
3. Has a higher per pupil cost than regular education.
4. Submits separate budgets in order to draw on federal, state, and local funds to meet these excess costs.
5. Seeks to provide education for a wider age-range of children (3-21 years) than does the regular program in most states.
6. Actively seeks to locate, identify, evaluate, and serve all handicapped children of school age.
7. Provides an individualized education program (IEP) for each student it serves. This program is reviewed and revised at least annually.

8. Provides related services which are not usually offered to the nonhandicapped, such as occupational therapy, special transportation, and parent counseling and training.

9. Provides special education and related services for private school handicapped children in the jurisdiction of the public school district.

10. Involves parents in their child's education as a legal requirement.

11. Provides specially trained personnel to serve the handicapped.

This is a formidable list. But we're not through yet. The services listed above pertain to special education only. There are other provisions for handicapped children which are similar to those in regular education, differing only in that more detail is involved in carrying out the special education responsibilities. Examples of this are in the detailed procedures for the confidentiality of special education information, and in planning for the handicapped to use regular school transportation. Thus the "special" part of your program includes not only those activities which are different from regular education, but also the indepth operation of services that both branches of education provide.

Tips on Handling Your Special Responsibilities

As administrator of special education, you will be concentrating on both aspects of the job, those that are distinct from regular education, and those that are the same but require more detail. You'll soon find that the same job in regular and special education can be worlds apart. Look at the business of pupil transportation.

Bus service for nonhandicapped students is worked out to accommodate the school routine, and to efficiently transport large groups of children who remain anonymous to the route-planner. Planning for handicapped children is a different matter. It is not enough to program a mentally retarded student into a transportation service. You must insure that the child learns the route from home to bus stop, that he or she is taught appropriate behavior on the bus, and that he or she benefits from the busing experience. (For many handicapped students, this is a vital part of education.)

Here is another kind of indepth service: A blind student, provided with the services of an itinerant teacher, may be considered by many as having his special education problem taken care of. Nothing is quite that simple. The administrator of special education must also insure that the child gets transported to school, that provisions are taken to insure that he will cross streets safely while going from home to bus stop, that he learns how to get to the lunchroom and other building facilities, and — perhaps most important — than an individualized education program is developed for the child. These provisions, which add up to a full education, mean that you, the special education administrator, must look at the handicapped child in reference to the total school environment. It is your responsibility to provide whatever is needed beyond that which is offered in the regular program in order for a child to receive an appropriate education.

The administrator of special education has broad vision. He consistently reviews the school life of the handicapped child, and at times the student's after-school life as well. Does a deaf student need counseling? Do the parents need counseling? Does a health-imparied child need further medical diagnosis? Is there a child in the district who is suspected of being handicapped? If the answer to these and similar questions is positive, then special help in the designated area is expected to be given.

Knowing Your Financial Resources

Let us assume you are knowledgeable about special education and have developed a good evaluation plan. Next, you begin to think about the special instruction and related services your district should provide; and you're brought up short against the problem of money. For many special education administrators the money shortage is the biggest hurdle of all. Excellent teachers are looking for jobs, fine instructional materials are for sale, and store shelves hold the best of special education equipment. Just about everything is available to implement an exemplary program — if you only had the money.

There are resources to help solve this dilemma. First of all, you have the money allotted to your program from district funds. Be conscientious in seeing that special education gets its share. Public Law 94-142, with its costly requirements, doesn't leave the district the option to spend or not to spend. Dollars, hundreds and sometimes thousands, will be necessary to provide every school-age handicapped child with an appropriate education.

A second source is state funding. Basic state school support is given for all school children, handicapped or not. In addition, states give further financial assistance to districts operating special education programs. This assistance must be applied for. The allocations vary, but in general it can be said that some of the special services a district offers are payable in part through state funding. If you're not sure which ones, check with your state educational agency. Many districts fail to do this and consequently put more expense on their local taxpayers than necessary, or fail to give as full a service as they could. The most common error is failing to claim full reimbursable amounts for special education materials, and for transportation. This won't apply to all states; the point is, though, to check and recheck until you are sure your program is funded as completely as possible. It's the mark of a good administrator.

Your third source of revenue is the federal government. The U.S. Department of Health, Education, and Welfare provides districts with financial support in three ways:

1. Federal flow-through money that comes to your district through your state educational agency. This includes a) the district's allocation of PL 94-142 funds, and b) the set-aside money for vocational and career education of the handicapped, required of recipients of federal money for regular vocational and career education. (There are other federal flow-through monies that aid the handicapped, such as Title I money for disadvantaged children who are also handicapped, and the national lunch program. But these programs do not have money set aside specifically for handicapped children.)

2. Support through services provided by a state agency, other than an education agency, and paid for, either in full or in part, with federal funds. An example of this is the service offered your high school handicapped by the Vocational Rehabilitation Division.

3. Support from federal grants made directly to your district. Under this system there have been Title III, Title IV, and Title VI-B monies, to name a few. PL 94-142, with its flow-through formula, has done away with some of the competitive grants for special education purposes. Should you

be interested in writing a grant for some specific project, contact your state office that has charge of federal projects and discuss your options.

Pointers on Budgeting

The administrator of special education has just finished talking to a large group of his district's regular and special educators. His address was inspiring. He told about all the improvements to be made in special education; classrooms that would permit better accessibility and use, individualized education programs, better transportation facilities, physical therapy and adaptive physical education programs. He went through the whole list of PL 94-142 requirements and ended on a note of such optimism that a spontaneous cheer went up from the audience.

Then a regular fifth grade teacher, young enough to be interested, yet old enough to be realistic, brought the response into practical focus when she jumped up and said, "Your plans are nifty-keen, sir, but they won't work. You won't have enough money."

Ah, money. You'll never have enough. But you wouldn't be an administrator if you didn't realize this already. Here are some tips to help you work within the confines of a budget:

1. A school district should organize its fiscal management system so that special education is a separate part of the district's budget.

2. The administrator of special education should have an active role in determining how fiscal resources for special education are to be budgeted and allocated.

3. Wherever possible, the monies allocated to special education should be based on the individual education needs of handicapped children, rather than on the category of the handicap, which is the traditional system. (So much allotted for the program for the mentally retarded, so much for the speech program, and so on.)

4. Program expenses should be clarified. Whose budget is responsible for widening toilet stall doors for a child in a wheelchair? Or for installing special door knobs and holding bars at the chalkboard, should a physically impaired child be programmed into a regular classroom?

5. A system which tracks item-by-item costs of all special education programs and services should be established. Consult people experienced in budget tracking and audit trails if you need to. The system should track expenses for:

a.	Childfind	e.	Staff Salaries
b.	Screening	f.	Equipment and Supplies
c.	Evaluation	g.	Purchased Services
d.	Medical Diagnosis	h.	Transportation

6. Undertake cost-effective action. Here are several examples of this:

   a. Contract with other school districts or private agencies for transportation, physical therapy, and other services, when the contracted cost is less than district cost for implementation.

   b. Enter into joint purchasing ventures with other districts. Districts report significant savings in cooperatively buying audiovisual equipment, art supplies by the gross, sheet music, and athletic equipment.

   c. Negotiate with vendors for delivery of school supplies during off-peak seasons. Large districts, especially, make substantial savings by checking when most districts are requesting delivery, then making their purchases at another time for a lowered price.

7. Investigate the services your SEA provides for your program. For example; don't set up an inservice for teachers out of your budget when your SEA has been granted federal funds explicitly for that purpose.

These seven tips are meant to get you started on thinking about how to stretch the dollars in your particular district. You'll come up with more opportunities to save, once you start moving along these lines.

Summary

The essential factor in special education is to provide for the unique needs of the handicapped. The administrator must be knowledgeable about these needs. He must understand what regular education should provide for the handicapped, and what his program should offer. To fulfill his program responsibilities, he has to be aware of his financial resources.

Chapter Two

Essential Jobs in Special Education Administration

Enjoy the comfort associated with being able to admit to some ignorance — it's much more fun to be helpable than infallible.

When you were hired, the school board looked to you as a person whose knowledge and leadership would be reflected in an exemplary special education program. In turn, you assumed responsibility for what goes on in special education in your district. Naturally, you want to do your best. So how do you go about it? Let's discuss some of the ways.

Visualizing Your District Needs

"How to visualize what your district needs to do," probably is a better statement. Here's a way to get a grasp on this overwhelming problem:

1. Compile a list of jobs that need doing. Include those jobs you're presently doing, such as handling transportation, as well as the jobs that will be done at a future date.
2. Break the list down into three categories and file properly:
   a. Tasks required by federal law under a federal heading.
   b. Tasks required by state laws and procedures (that are

not duplicates of federal requirements) under a state-law heading. You can make cross-references if you wish.

c. Tasks required by your district's unique policies and procedures, under your district heading.

This three-file system has a number of benefits:

1. You have easily accessible information concerning the requirements of federal, state, and local agencies.

2. The requirements are filed separately.

3. Each of the three files will be set up to enable you to retrieve information easily.

4. Duplications of requirements are easily seen if you employ a cross-reference system.

5. You can keep a record of the number of times you work out of each file.

6. You can keep a record of the number of hours spent on particular jobs in each file.

7. You have data to support the time spent on all job requirements.

8. As additional tasks become necessary, you file them in the proper category.

9. You have the data necessary for prioritizing jobs.

10. The three-file system helps guard against spending too much on any one of the three agencies.

This last item needs some discussion. We put it in because in an era of federal intervention in special education if all tasks are lumped into one file you might find yourself dealing with federal requirements most of the day without realizing it. And this isn't the way it should be. Your district's policies and customs deserve their percentage of your time also. Law takes precedence over custom, but it shouldn't exclude it. If your district's unique procedures are disregarded you'll soon discover you're losing out on much of the support your community would normally give. One administrator posed the problem of retaining local practices in a way that reflects the concerns of many:

"It's a practice in my community to have parent group meetings," he said, "but with all this work to be done under PL 94-142 should I take time to provide for these meetings, too?"

By all means. Make them part of a yearly plan. In point of fact, the meetings can even help in the implementation of PL 94-142.

Another example of a district custom is arranging for handicapped children to attend summer camp. There is no law saying a district shall do this, yet what administrator who accepts the responsibility to provide this fine service would fail to enhance his administrative role — and the lives of many handicapped children. It's a good item to put in your district file. Use your district file, it's a solid step toward success.

How to State Your Objectives

As you compile your three files of federal, state, and local needs, you may find it helpful to state them in the form of objectives. There is no regulation saying this must be done. If it suits your situation better to have the jobs stated as work activities, then do so. However, for many administrators a list of behaviorally stated objectives is the ideal way to write down program requirements.

A behavioral objective defines the conditions that will exist when the objective is attained. For example, your district has been educating handicapped children aged 6-18 years. Now PL 94-142 mandates that you educate a wider age range. The new objective can be stated in two ways. As a simple work activity, *"We have to provide special education for all handicapped children, 3-21 years, by 1982."* Or as a behavioral statement, *"All handicapped children, 3-21 years, receive special education in 1982 and thereafter."* Here you state the behavior that is going to exist in 1982. You describe what is going to happen, and now it is up to you to make it come about. Behavioral objectives are strong statements. They force us to action.

Remember that objectives or goals (the two terms are often used interchangeably) are attainments which are *sought;* therefore the statement of them doesn't place you under a binding contract. This is important for persons who hesitate to write in behavioral terms because they think they will be legally bound under them. What is expected is a commitment to attain the objectives as completely as possible, and within the time allotted.

In stating your objectives be sure you have a complete set. At some time or another, a person might judge your program by the information revealed in your goal statements. State them on a chart or in a brochure about your special education program, or have them listed in the three-file system we've talked about. The point is to have them written down, and accessible.

Tips on Prioritizing

We can't do everything at once, so we prioritize. The criteria for this task depend on two ingredients. One is the time factor; the other involves the importance of the job that needs doing. Looking at "time" first, let us examine this situation:

> You are part of a team which evaluates special education teaching materials. Next week is the deadline for reviewing a certain supplemental reading series some teachers want to begin to use. The team sent the material to you for your review a week before the final meeting. This isn't the most important job that you're faced with; so you let it slide. The time runs out and you'll not have another chance to do your part as a team member. If you had studied the time factor this wouldn't have happened to you.

The factor of "importance" in reference to prioritizing involves time, also. But it's more than that. A job termed very important, or "top priority," usually means that if the job isn't done the agency will suffer significant setbacks.

To rank jobs you need information about them. In the federal field:

1. You need to keep up-to-date on federal rules and regulation. Your state educational agency should be assisting in this. If they aren't, get in touch with them and tell them they're not.

2. You need to understand federal requirements in the order of their importance. This will be discussed in a number of sections in this book. Meanwhile, here are examples of top priority items under PL 94-142:

   a. The need for each child being served in special education to have an Individualized Education Program (IEP).

b. The need to develop procedures for your district's child-census program.

Your priority list regarding state statutes necessitates this information:

1. Input from your state educational agency (SEA) regarding state laws and rules.
2. Procedures and criteria for determining which children are eligible for special education and related services.
3. What is involved in filing a claim for your district's share in the state reimbursement program.

When prioritizing your file of local policies and customs, you're on your own. There are no laws to steer by. Here are some guidelines:

1. Consider the traditional jobs your community feels are important.
2. Include those jobs not being done but which you feel are important for your district.

At times district innovations require creativity and perseverance. For example:

You have an idea for a better way to utilize the planning days granted to your teachers each year. Get your idea down on paper, talk it over with your staff, field test it on a mini-scale if you can. And if it proves to be worth the effort, prioritize its implementation. There may be some inertia on your part, and maybe some resistance on your staff's, but put these hindrances aside and go full steam ahead if you're convinced that the attainment of your objective will measurably improve your program. The point is, don't confine all your activity to carrying out directives from above. Give yourself time to grow as a true leader.

Top Priorities Without Timelines

There are some items that we don't prioritize and that have no timeline, but nevertheless are of major importance. We keep them in mind no matter what job we're doing. An example: Keeping operating costs at a minimum.

This doesn't mean you cut the quality of the service in order to cut the cost. Rather, it means to offer the best service within the cost range that is the most economical for your district.

> Let's say the district has been purchasing special education services for its severely mentally retarded children from an adjoining district. The program is a good one; however, one of your objectives has been to bring these students back into their home district. You discover that the cost of implementing a comparable program in your district would far exceed the purchased cost. So for the time being you remove this objective from your priority list.

Keeping costs at a minimum is just one example of a top priority that's almost never written down but always at work. Here are other responsibilities which always get top attention:

1. Responding to student emergencies.
2. Evaluating and responding accordingly to parent communications.
3. Responding to teachers' requests for help.
4. Evaluating and responding accordingly to criticism of your district's special education program. If the criticism is aired through public media, this media should be used in your response.
5. Responding to emergencies and other problems brought to your attention by your superior.

Other examples of top priority may be of a more personal nature. For example, an administrator of special education who wishes to enhance his opportunity for advancement may seek occasions to speak in public about his program. Another may have as top priority the improvement of his relationship with his school board. It's a good suggestion to write down your top priority personal goals, and the steps to be taken for their accomplishment.

Developing a
Dynamic Organization Chart

The organization chart, or plan, brings a number of things together — the special education staff, the positions they hold, and the jobs performed under the positions. This is the one place where your whole special education operation is visible at a glance. We suggest you draw up your chart in the form of a matrix. Figure 2-1 illustrates what is meant.

Examining the chart, you will notice that the left hand column is headed Special Education and Related Services. We have entered four general components in this column. You may want to change this to a list of particular services on your chart:

1. Special transportation
2. Psychological services
3. Counseling services
4. Parent meetings
5. Child census
6. Personnel development
7. etc.

On the other hand, some administrators will combine more than one service into a single statement. For instance, the Least Restrictive Environment item can go with the Individualized Education Program since the environment is decided during the development of the IEP. You are the judge as to how long this column will be. Just be careful not to leave out any service you provide. All answers to inquiries about what special services and related operations are offered in your program should be able to be located on the chart, either as separate entries or implied under related ones.

The row across the top of the matrix states the job titles of the special education staff. These positions don't have to be full time in special education. If your regular school psychologist works part time on the evaluation of handicapped children, he should be included — as should the school counselors for the handicapped, the health nurse, and the adaptive physical education instructor.

Extending lines downward from the sections across the top, and drawing lines across from the left hand column, you form the matrix boxes. Entered in these boxes are the duties staff members perform for the appropriate service.

Our sample chart illustrates a small operation. A large district may require a multi-organization chart, actually three or more charts in one. Build them in the same way shown in the illustration. One chart can present the overall district organization of special

Figure 2-1
SPECIAL EDUCATION ORGANIZATION CHART

SERVICES	PERSONAL RESPONSIBILITIES				
Special Education and Related Services	Administrator	Resource Rooms Staff	Speech and Itinerant Staff (Blind, etc.)	Psychologist	Support Staff: Counselor, Nurse, OT, PT
1. Location, Identification, Screening	Develop format Implement Report	Participate as per speciality	Participate	Evaluate students for special services	Participate as per speciality
2. Individualized Education Program (IEP)	Organize team Conduct meetings Provide all-district inservice Monitor implementation	Team member Evaulation input Help develop, review, revise, and implement	Team member Evaluation input Help develop, review, revise and implement	Team member and/or re-source person	Present input Resource person Help implement

3. Student Instruction	Methods and materials leadership Individual aid Supervision Parent Involvement	Teach toward individual goals Progress records Parent reporting Liaison with regular education	Organize scheduling Teach toward goals Report to parents and regular teachers	Resource for learning modalities Test interpretation	Set scheduling Report student progress
4. Least Restrictive Environment	All-district inservice Resource person for implementation Monitor	Input at child's IEP meeting Help monitor	Input at child's IEP meeting Help monitor	Input at child's IEP meeting	Input for placement and monitoring

education; the left hand column will list the responsibility areas, the top row will show the staff, and the boxes will state the jobs to be performed. A second chart can delineate the organization of the program for the deaf, for example. A third might present the learning disabled program, a fourth, the program provided for students in the resource rooms. There will be a certain amount of overlap in these charts, since many of the same services are provided in each category of handicapping condition.

Work with your chart (or charts) until you are satisfied it can aid you in:

1. Explaining your job.
2. Presenting your program to others.
3. Explaining to individual staff members their part in the overall special education operation.
4. Comparing job loads of staff members. (This item can be broken out of the organization chart and developed in depth where necessary.)
5. Presenting an organized listing of the array of services provided by your program.
6. Comparing services offered in the various categories of exceptionality. The numbers of handicapped children provided for and the severity of the handicapping condition in each category would also be involved in this comparison.

When you are satisfied that your chart can stand the test of time and use, arrange it in a final format, realizing, though, that because it is a *dynamic* instrument, you will be changing it from time to time.

Tying up the Whole Package

The package of special education can never be permanently signed, sealed, and delivered. The program is constantly expanding, new laws are enacted, and the delivery system fluctuates. For example:

A few years ago the self-contained classroom was considered the ideal environment for the education of the handicapped. Today every eligible child receives his special education services in the regular program unless it can be shown that a more restricted environment is better.

The closest you can come to tying up a package is to plan a course of action over a period of time; for example, during a school year. And then see that the plans made for that year are completed. That's the package we're talking about.

A school year usually starts with a number of new responsibilities, as well as the traditional jobs that must be done. Set up your files of things to be accomplished and begin prioritizing as soon as your work year starts. Set timelines on those items that require them. Take charge of your time from the outset. If you don't, it will take charge of you. Without organization, your year will be strewn with half-finished projects, and you'll end it with a number of loose ends trailing the close of school. Avoid this dissipation by planning your work, and mentally tie up each particular job, or part of a job, as it is completed.

Psychologically speaking, it is better to do this without a lot of fanfare. You don't want your plans to turn into a game where colleagues watch you meet or beat your deadlines. Your reputation for getting things done will emerge of its own accord as your staff experiences your stability and the completeness with which you accomplish each particular job you undertake.

Thus far we've talked about your efforts in developing a year's work package for your program. The fact that special education is part of a much larger package, the district operation, must not be overlooked. Figure 2-2 is a partial illustration of a district plan, showing what may be expected from the district's administrator of special education.

We suggest you utilize the information given in Figure 2-2 to evaluate your own program's chart. As you note the responsibilities listed under your position title, ask yourself these questions:

1. Does my operational chart reflect the administrative responsibilities assigned me by my district?

2. Is there evidence of program planning on my operational chart?

3. Are all the requirements of PL 94-142, and our state laws, included in my chart?

4. Have I included staff inservice, evaluation, and program assistance?

5. Does my chart reflect my liaison responsibilities with the central office and regular education?

Figure 2-2
PARTIAL VIEW OF
DISTRICT ORGANIZATION CHART
(illustrating responsibilities
of Director of Special Education)

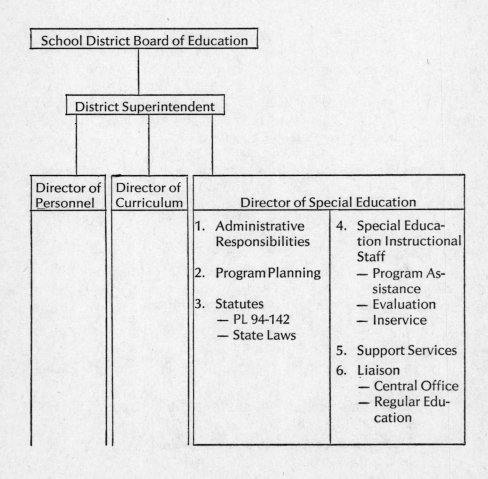

Summary

It is essential that the administrator of special education understand what is to be done under PL 94-142, under his state statutes, and in accordance with district customs and needs. The jobs in these three categories should be prioritized. The administrator must develop a dynamic organization chart which reflects his total special education operation.

Chapter Three

How Public Law 94-142 Affects a District

When you're through changing, you're through.

A new dimension has been added to the administration of special education. Federal law is in the picture. With the signing of PL 94-142 every school district in the nation is responsible for provisions in special education which were optional, or unheard of, a few years ago.

Public Law 94-142 amends Part B of the Education of the Handicapped Act (EHA). The new amendments are designed to:

1. Assure that all handicapped children have available to them a free, appropriate education.
2. Assist states and local districts to provide for the education of handicapped children.
3. Assure that the rights of handicapped children and their parents are protected.

The Power Behind the Law

The enabling force behind PL 94-142 lies in three areas. First of all, it's the law of the land and must be obeyed. Second, the important requirements in PL 94-142 closely parallel the requirements in Section 504, Subpart D, of the Rehabilitation Act of 1973. This act amends the Civil Rights Act of 1964 and is being vigorously enforced, according to the Secretary of the Department of Health, Education, and Welfare. The third force behind PL 94-142 is the financial impact. School districts need the funds the law provides; therefore they act in compliance with the funding source.

A national trend toward better education for the handicapped could be mentioned as a fourth force. Within the last half-dozen years, districts desiring to establish or uphold an exemplary standing in current educational practices have seen the need to provide a more appropriate education for their handicapped students. Advocacy groups can take credit for this. Public Law 94-142 hasn't come to us cold. It's the legal answer to demands made by militant people working together for the rights of the handicapped over a number of years.

How National Uniformity Helps Administrators

One of the results of PL 94-142 is the unified approach, on a national scale, in implementing local programs. For better or for worse, we are operating much of the time under one set of extensive federal laws. PL 94-142 reaches into every aspect of special education and demands nearly uniform responses. The federal definitions of the handicapping conditions are used by everyone. We may not fully agree with them, but they do reduce confusion. For the first time, we are speaking a common language when discussing education of the handicapped.

Emerging national uniformity in special education has accomplished a further end. It permits a handbook, such as this, to be a useful and specific guide for every administrator of special education in the country. Writing for a national audience, we can say that every school district in our nation now implements the following general requirements mandated by PL 94-142:

1. A free, appropriate education for all handicapped children.
2. A system to locate and identify handicapped children.
3. An evaluation for every child known to be, or suspected of being, handicapped.
4. The development of an individualized education program for every handicapped child.
5. A system to insure confidentiality of records.
6. A system to protect the rights of children, parents, and guardians.

These six items are the meat of PL 94-142. They must be worked into your district plan.

What Goes into Your District Plan Under PL 94-142

Your district's responsibilities relative to PL 94-142 are discussed in detail in various parts of this book. An introductory list is given here. These are the specific topics you deal with in implementing PL 94-142:

1. Procedures which insure that all children residing within the jurisdiction of your school district who are handicapped, or suspected of being handicapped, are identified, located, and evaluated.

2. Policies and procedures which insure confidentiality of personally identifiable information pertaining to handicapped children.

3. A goal of providing full educational opportunity to all handicapped children, aged 3 through 21 (or of an age which qualifies them for public schooling under your state statutes), and a timetable for accomplishing this goal.

4. A description of the kind and number of facilities, personnel, and services necessary to meet the goal of providing full educational opportunity to all handicapped children.

5. Procedures to help implement, and use, the comprehensive system of personnel development established by your state educational agency in compliance with PL 94-142.

6. Procedures to identify, locate, evaluate, and provide an appropriate education for handicapped children who are not receiving any education at all. These children are termed "first priority."

7. Procedures for improving the education provided for "second priority children." These are children, within each disability, who have the most severe handicaps and who are currently receiving an inadequate education.

8. Procedures to encourage the participation of parents or guardians of handicapped children in the development of

their child's individualized education program (IEP). Records must be kept of efforts to involve parents.

9. Procedures to insure that your district provides special education services in a way which permits handicapped children to participate in regular educational programs to the maximum extent practicable.

10. Assurance that the funds provided under PL 94-142 for your district's use are expended in a manner which complies with the regulations under PL 94-142.

11. A description of how your district will use the funds granted under PL 94-142 during each successive school year.

12. Assurance that your district is providing services which, taken as a whole, are equally effective for all handicapped children in the district. The district-wide services must be of comparable quality. Example: speech therapy cannot be offered in some schools and not in others where there are children who need this service.

13. Sufficient information to enable your state educational agency to monitor your district's special education program under PL 94-142.

14. Records that demonstrate the correctness and verification of the information your district furnishes your state educational agency under PL 94-142.

15. Provisions for making your district's application for funds under PL 94-142, and all documents related to the application, available to parents and the general public. Notice of this availability shall be given in newspapers or other media.

16. Procedures to assure that your district is complying with PL 94-142 in developing and implementing an individualized education program (IEP) for each of its handicapped students.

17. Assurance that all policies and programs which your district establishes and administers, other than those under PL 94-142, are consistent with PL 94-142.

18. Assurance that your district has procedural safeguards which meet the requirements under PL 94-142.

19. Assurance that your district is making positive efforts to employ, and advance in employment, qualified handicapped

individuals. Many districts have already filed this assurance since it is required of all programs that are assisted by HEW, under Title 45 of the Code of Federal Regulations, Part 84, A reference to the assurance already filed will suffice.

20. Additional procedures and information which your state educational agency may require in order to complete the state's annual program plan. This plan, under PL 94-142, is submitted each year by your SEA to the United States Commissioner of Education for approval for state funding.

The above items comprise the responsibilities for the local education agency, under PL 94-142. They are written as twenty concise statements, but it will take this entire book to describe their implementation. Before launching into this task, we'll talk about unforeseen things that affect a district because of PL 94-142.

What to Watch for When Implementing the Federal Law

The goals and objectives under PL 94-142 are numerous enough to just about eliminate any others. But not *all* others. We remind you that each district has its unique practices; watch out that they aren't lost in the shuffle. Recall, too, that you are working with and for people, including members of your school board, who may never have heard of PL 94-142. Don't sweep the rug out from under them with a rush to make the federal requirements take the place of everything the district has built up over the years.

Another item to watch for: You may become so used to following federal regulations that you lose sight of the fact you are also a leader, and a developer of ideas. There are channels in which you can exercise your initiative when implementing PL 94-142. Here are some examples:

1. Developing your district's systems for implementing PL 94-142 — take pride in doing this well.
2. Developing a community vocational training program for handicapped students.
3. Convening a multi-district administrators' conference in order to discuss common problems.

Our final watchword: As time goes on, the implementation of

PL 94-142 will become routine. It will blend with all your other routine duties. Meanwhile, a number of requirements under the new law are still causing some consternation. The following reports from administrators in the field may prepare you, especially those new to the job, on what to expect as the law gains momentum.

1. A district of 22,000 school children has had to hire a special education person to do nothing but work on the development of the individualized education programs for its handicapped children.

2. An administrator of special education states, "It was bad enough when we had to get parent permission to give a child a psychological test. Now we have to have written permission for the whole battery of evaluation instruments and parents have to know what they're signing. So we go through a summary of the tests for each parent. It isn't that I disagree with this. The problem is that it takes so much time."

3. A director of special education reports that the call on his staff's time increased tremendously when the parochial school principals in his district, after a workshop on PL 94-142, requested full evaluation of all children suspected of being handicapped.

4. Another administrator voiced a concern that's all too common. "My application for PL 94-142 funds requires me to sign an assurance that our district has done all in its power to locate all first priority children. (Those not receiving any education at all.) If some first priority children are later located, will I, or my district, be vulnerable for litigation?"

Other reports included these problems:

1. Some regular teachers are disconcerted because of the disproportionate number of students they have, compared to special teachers.

2. Transfers to special education are bogged down due to the time it takes to cover all eligibility requirements.

3. Parents complain about having to sign so many papers.

4. Some parents are requesting more and more information, putting an extra load on the special education administrator.

As can be seen from these examples, the implementation of PL 94-142 isn't easy. There are no pat answers to the problems stated above. The law is too ambitious and, alas, at times too ambiguous, to be easily fitted into a district operation.

The Impact of PL 94-142 on the Child

The essential impact of the law is not what the district has to do. Rather, it is the impact on the children for whom the law was enacted. Under provisions of PL 94-142, handicapped children:

1. Are assured that their unique needs will be taken care of — the result of efforts to actively seek them out for purposes of identifying their condition, evaluating their potential, and providing them with an appropriate education.

2. Are assured that they can reach their potential to a high degree — a result of their complete evaluation and correct educational placement.

3. Are taking an active part in their classes — the result of the IEP, which places them in programs suited to their needs and capabilities.

4. Have the satisfaction that federal, state, and local funds are available to help pay the excess cost of their education.

5. Do not have to compete in classes beyond their ability — the result of an IEP.

6. Are not removed from the school's mainstream unless it can be shown that an alternate setting would be more beneficial.

7. Are receiving counseling, along with their parents, when the need is indicated.

8. Are assured that architectural barriers no longer impede their movement about their school and campus — a result of laws prohibiting barriers that prevent normal movement by the handicapped.

9. Are assured their parents are informed about the child's progress, and are involved in their educational planning.

10. Are assured that they will be transported to and from school, even if special vehicles are required.

11. Are assured they won't be excluded from such classes as physical education and vocational training because of their handicap. Their instruction has to be specially designed.

These are some obvious impacts of the law on our handicapped children. The improvement in self-image when receiving an education in the mainstream and the increase in self-confidence from being placed in programs they can handle are intangible results.

Tips on Jobs Involving Your State Educational Agency

The tasks we describe here involve information you send to your SEA as you carry out PL 94-142.

First, you provide your state agency with the information it needs to fulfill reporting obligations to the U.S. Commissioner of Education. For example, the child census report. Your district is locating and identifying children as a regular part of its operation, but periodically a formal report will be made concerning these activities. This reporting, and other information requested by your SEA, are needed in order for the SEA's annual plan to be approved by the federal government. Approval of a state's plan means that state can begin to receive flow-through funds under PL 94-142.

Secondly, you submit a formal application to your state educational agency for your district's share of flow-through money under PL 94-142. The application requires a detailed description of how your district plans to utilize these federal funds.

It's the responsibility of the SEA to establish the general procedures and suggest a format for local educational agencies to use in preparing their application. Your job is to follow the directives and get your application in on time. Your SEA will evaluate your application, giving special attention to that part which describes how you plan to use the funds. The State Agency has to be careful in this evaluation because they, in turn, are monitored by the Federal Bureau for the Education of the Handicapped (BEH). Should an SEA be at fault in its evaluation of an application and award money to a district which is not in compliance with PL 94-142, the whole state funding under PL 94-142 may suffer.

When a district is in noncompliance with PL 94-142, the SEA can cut off funds for that district. When the SEA, itself, is found to be in noncompliance with PL 94-142, the total state funds, under PL 94-142, can be cut off at the federal source.

Should your district choose not to apply for funding under PL 94-142, the district administration should direct special attention to the regulations under Section 504 of the Rehabilitation Act of

1973. These regulations closely parallel those under PL 94-142. The Rehabilitation Act is considered a Civil Rights law; its rules must be complied with whether funding under PL 94-142 is sought or not. A district can choose not to apply for funds under PL 94-142, but it has no choice in providing a free, appropriate education for all handicapped children. PL 94-142 and Section 504 of the Rehabilitation Act both mandate this provision.

It is one of the special education administrator's duties to bring all these ramifications of the law to the attention of the appropriate district personnel, and to see that compliance with these federal laws is met.

Chapter Four

Key Information
About Handicapped Children

See your special education students as in the process of becoming, as growing, improving human beings...just as you have been seen by others who gambled once or twice on your potential.

A start toward providing full education opportunity for the handicapped is the acquisition of special education information. In tune with the rest of this book, only the essentials are given here, with further sources of information for those interested. Some items cut across all categories. Three important ones are discussed below.

What's Being Done for All

These services potentially involve all handicapped children. The first service is the free, appropriate education which is discussed throughout this book. Second, handicapped children in school districts that receive any financial assistance from the U.S. Department of Health Education, and Welfare, must be provided with an education in compliance with Section 504 of the Rehabilitation Act of 1973. As we mentioned in Chapter 3, the requirements of Section 504 (a civil rights law) closely parallel those of PL 94-142.

The third service states that all handicapped children, regardless of age, can be applicants for Supplemental Security Income (SSI) under Public Law 92-603. You should refer parents to their nearest social security office for information about this assistance. The people there will help them with the application. Persons who qualify for the program receive monthly cash payments from the government. It is important to pass this information on, as a report from Washington, D.C. states that SSI is underused. It is failing to provide cash assistance to as many as 80 percent of eligible children. The following involves financial savings for parents.

Tax Deductions and Other Legal Rights

For information about tax deductions for the care of their handicapped child, parents can write for a booklet, "Facts You Should Know About Tax Deductions for Your Handicapped Child." The address is:

Coordinating Council for Handicapped Children
407 South Dearborn
Chicago, ILL 60605

For information concerning the legal rights of the handicapped, write to:

National Center for Law and the Handicapped, Inc.
1235 North Eddy Street
South Bend, Indiana 46617

Another source of information on legal rights is:

Council for Exceptional Children
1920 Association Drive
Reston, Virginia 22091

Closer Look is a periodical which serves two purposes. First, it provides general information on all handicapping conditions, including the handicapped person's legal rights. Second, parents and professionals can write to *Closer Look* for assistance in dealing with particular problems and needs of mentally, physically, or emotionally disabled children. In writing about a child be specific, include facts about the person's age, handicap, and the kind of help being sought. The response will be an appropriate packet that includes suggestions on getting the service the child needs, organizations to contact, facts about laws and rights, and reading that can help parents and professionals. All *Closer Look* services and publications are free of charge. It is published by the U.S. Department of Health, Education, and Welfare. To put your name on the mailing list write to:

> Closer Look
> Box 1492
> Washington, D.C. 20013

In addition to these general assistance items, there are services offered to specific groups of handicapped.

The Vocational Rehabilitation Program

Vocational Rehabilitation for the Disabled is administered by the Federal Rehabilitation Service Administration. Services include counseling and guidance, medical examination and help, physical aids such as glasses and hearing aids, job training, job placement, and follow-up. The program usually serves young handicapped adults, sixteen years or older, who are seeking employment. Vocational Rehabilitation works in accord with your State Vocational Rehabilitation Agency. Information is available at any Social Security or Vocational Rehabilitation Office. School personnel, as well as parents, will be interested in this service.

Tips on Employment Possibilities

The employable handicapped population of America, between the ages of 16 and 65, numbers nearly 12,000,000 according to the latest census report. The outlook for employment has improved in recent years; however, there are still over 7,000,000 unemployed handicapped Americans who are willing to go to work. Factors which will contribute toward the reduction of this number include improvements in the educational process, attitudinal changes in society, removal of architectural barriers, and further legislative action.

The Division of Vocational Rehabilitation, mentioned above, and Goodwill Industries are examples of agencies offering rehabilitation services, training, and employment for the handicapped throughout the country. Goodwill's national address is:

> Goodwill Industries, Inc.
> 9200 Wisconsin Avenue
> Washington, D.C. 20014

One of the best resources for employment of the handicapped is your high school work-experience program. When properly implemented, this program provides the student with:

1. Evaluation which determines the kinds of jobs he'll succeed in.
2. On-the-job training experience.
3. Placement in competitive, or subsidized, employment before leaving school.

Employment of the handicapped is one of your program's main goals, and also one of the most difficult to attain. Give all the time that's needed to your work-experience program. An administrator of special education can't be completely successful until the students who pass through his program are appropriately employed in some capacity.

The Four Developmental Disabilities

At times the administrator of special education will be asked questions regarding children with developmental disabilities. These disabilities include the four conditions of *mental retardation, cerebral palsy, epilepsy,* and *autism.* Developmental disability is not mentioned in PL 94-142, but the four conditions are dealt with. Mental retardation has its own category in PL 94-142; cerebral palsy and epilepsy are listed in the "Orthopedically and Other Health Impaired" category; and autism is under "Seriously Emotionally Disturbed."

According to the accepted definition, a developmental disability originates before age 18, continues indefinitely, and constitutes a substantial handicap. A federal law (PL 94-103), titled the Developmental Disabled Assistance and Bill of Rights Act, guarantees that developmentally disabled persons have a right to "appropriate treatment, services, and habilitation." For further information write to:

U.S. Department of Health, Education, and Welfare
Office of Human Development
Developmental Disabilities Office
Washington, D.C. 20201

Since mental retardation is dealt with later on in this book (see Chapter 5), we'll present here some vital facts on the remaining three developmental disabilities:

1. *Epilepsy:* This term applies to disorders of the central nervous system characterized by seizures. About 4,000,000 people in the United States have this affliction. Epilepsy can result from defects in the brain; brain injury before, during, or after birth; head injuries; chemical imbalance; poor nutrition; childhood fevers; some infectious diseases; brain tumors; and some poisons.

The three types of seizures are: (A) Grand Mal, which lasts a few minutes or more and occurs one or more times daily, weekly, monthly, or annually. The victim loses consciousness and has convulsions. (B) Petit Mal, most common in children. The seizures last from 5 to 20 seconds and can occur many times an hour. Petit Mal can be accompanied by staring or twitching of the eyelids and momentary lapse of consciousness. (C) Psychomotor seizures, which occur at any age and have a complex behavior pattern including chewing and lip-smacking, staring and confusion, headaches, changes in color perception, spots before eyes, fear, anger, and, following the seizure, sleep.

Epilepsy cannot be cured, although childhood epilepsy will sometimes disappear in later years. Medication controls the disorder. People with epilepsy often need services such as counseling, special education for those with poorly controlled seizures, and special living arrangements. It is important to note that the affliction usually doesn't affect a person's intelligence. For further information write to:

> Epilepsy Foundation of America
> 1828 L Street, N.W.
> Washington, D.C. 20036

2. *Cerebral Palsy:* Cerebral palsy (CP) is not a single disorder but a group of dysfunctions having a variety of symptoms. There are three main types: The spastic person moves stiffly and with difficulty. The athetoid has involuntary and uncontrolled movements. The ataxic has a disturbed sense of balance and depth perception. About 750,000 people in the United States have this affliction.

Any damage to brain tissue can cause cerebral palsy. It can be the result of defective development, disease, or an injury occurring any time in pre-birth or life. A chief cause is insufficient oxygen reaching the fetal or newborn brain. Where braces, hearing aids, glasses, or other devices are necessary, early use — well before kindergarten age — can be of great help in the child's progress. Guidance is needed during schooling to help persons cope with their disability. Cerebral palsy is not always associated with mental retardation. There are persons with CP in almost every type of occupation from the lowest job to professional careers. For further information write to:

> United Cerebral Palsy Association
> 66 E. 34th Street
> New York, NY 10016

3. *Autism:* Autism refers to severe disorders of communication and behavior. The universal symptom is the child's inability to relate to others in a normal way. Common characteristics include non-response to sounds, a total lack of interest in other persons, staring into space, failure to use speech effectively, rocking or other repetitive behaviors, and tantrums. Autistic children have been known to show above normal skill in some isolated areas such as mathematics and music performance. Autism is found throughout the world and in every social class. About 100,000 people in the United States have this affliction. Some research suggests the cause might be a metabolic disorder. There is no known cure.

The mainstays of treatment are parental guidance, special education and vocational training, psychotherapy, and institutional treatment. In recent years teams of people have combined aspects of behavior modification, psychotherapy, and educational methods into a treatment that has produced dramatic changes in some children and noticeable improvement in many. For further information write to:

> National Society for Autistic Children
> 169 Tampa Avenue
> Albany, NY 12208

The Appropriately Educated Child

During the early days of PL 94-142 there was considerable concern about the meaning of "appropriate education." At one time, in fact, some high-powered educators, having gone to Washington, D.C.

to help unravel the requirements implied in the term, were given the task of coming up with a definition. After struggling for days, the group finally arrived at a statement which sounded so much like a dictionary it was decided to leave the definition to the wordmen and get along with the more important problem of what comprises an appropriate education. Using this approach, a handicapped child is said to have an appropriate education under the following circumstances:

1. His impairment is identified and its adverse effects alleviated as far as possible. This includes alleviation of physical impairments that affect his learning and overall development:

    a. He has recourse to medical services, provided by a licensed physician, to determine his medically related handicapping condition, if any.

    b. When a hearing loss is suspected, his hearing is evaluated. If necessary, the school provides habilitative activities such as language habilitation, auditory training, and lip reading. If needed, a hearing aid is selected and periodically evaluated as to its efficiency.

    c. When vision loss is suspected, his eyes are examined and steps taken to correct or alleviate the problem. Residual impairments are compensated for by large print books, Braille writing, and itinerant teacher service.

    d. He receives the school health services which are described under the school nurse's job.

    e. He has the specialized equipment and facilities he needs to participate in a beneficial education program. Examples include a specially designed school bus, ramps, lifts, and special play and classroom equipment.

    f. Physical therapy (PT) is available and provided by a qualified physical therapist.

    g. Occupational Therapy (OT) is available and includes improving, developing, or restoring functions imparied or lost through illness, injury, or deprivation; and preventing, through early intervention, initial or further impairment of functions.

2. He is provided with counseling services given by qualified

social workers, psychologists, guidance counselors, or other qualified personnel.

3. He is provided with recreation services which include assessment of leisure facilities, therapeutic recreation services, and leisure time education.

4. He is provided with social work services which include:

   a. Preparing a social or developmental history on the child.

   b. Group and individual counseling with the child and family.

   c. Working with problems in his living situation (home, school, and community) that affect his adjustment in school.

   d. Mobilizing school and community resources to enable him to receive maximum benefit from his education.

5. Speech pathology services are available and include:

   a. Procedures to identify speech or language disorders.

   b. Diagnosis and appraisal of his specific disorders.

   c. Referral for medical or other professional attention necessary for the habilitation of his disorders.

   d. Provision of services for the habilitation of his communication disorders.

   e. Counseling and guidance regarding speech and language disorders.

The above provisions are in the Related Services section in the regulations under PL 94-142. Here are some excerpts from the PL 94-142 Senate Committee Report which accompanied these regulations, and which have particular importance to administrators of special education: "The list of related services is not exhaustive and may include other developmental, corrective, or supportive services (such as artistic and cultural programs, and art, music, and dance therapy), if they are required to assist a handicapped child to benefit from special education." A second comment by the same committee states, "Each related service defined under this part may include appropriate administrative and supervisory activities that are necessary for program planning, management, and evaluation."

The following essentials pertain more directly to the special education program, as distinguished from the related services mentioned above. This aspect of an appropriate education requires that:

6. The child has an individualized education program (IEP) developed and implemented to meet his unique needs. Provisions under the IEP include assessment and evaluation, parent involvement, and a statement of student goals, and related services to be given.

7. The school district has developed a plan to identify his need for special education as early as possible in his life.

8. The district assists his parents in understanding his special needs. Parents are provided with information about child development.

9. His education is provided in the regular setting, unless he isn't able to profit from this environment — in which case he is assigned to the least restrictive alternate setting in which he can profit.

10. In non-academic settings (lunch, recess, etc.) he participates with non-handicapped children to the maximum extent appropriate to his needs.

11. He is provided with the same services that other special education students have who have the same disability and are in his age group.

12. He has available to him the educational programs and services available to non-handicapped children in his school district. These include art, music, industrial arts, consumer and homemaking education, and vocational education.

13. He has available to him extracurricular services such as athletics, special interest clubs, and referral to helping agencies.

14. His education includes a physical education program, especially designed if necessary.

15. The personnel who carry out his IEP are qualified to do so by training and proper certification.

16. Procedural safeguards, as required under PL 94-142, are in effect and include these assurances:

   a. His parents' written consent is obtained before the district conducts a preplacement evaluation, places him in special education, or releases any of his personally identifiable records.

   b. His native language is used for communication when this proves the most efficient method for him and his parents.

    c. When it is demonstrated that he needs his specially designed education delivered by an agency other than his own district, his district will provide and pay for such education.

All of the above provisions are requirements under PL 94-142. Thus, a district provides an appropriate education for a handicapped student when these services are available to him as needed.

Tips on Tests and Texts

To draft an appropriate individualized curriculum means that a great deal must be known about the child. Two sources yield this information. One is teacher and parent observation and teacher-made tests. The other is a standardized testing program. Eight areas that should be explored during assessment and evaluation are:

1. Mental Ability
2. Achievement and Readiness
3. Behavior and Development
4. Speech and Language
5. Reading
6. Mathematics
7. Spelling
8. Occupational Interest

Testing in these areas informs the teacher and the administrator of special education of the student's present level of academic and psychomotor functioning, his interests and abilities, his adaptive social behavior rating, and his weaknesses and strengths within any one basic area (such as math, reading, or spelling). For a title and description of appropriate tests in each area, consult the current Buros, Mental Measurement Yearbook.

After assessment is accomplished (see Chapter 11 for details), we come to the selection of textbooks. Teachers should be aware that students with academic problems often need a learning ladder of small, carefully structured steps. This is particularly true in reading. There are texts which introduce new sounds and words in a comfortable context before the child is expected to read them in the story. Other series do not, relying on the "transfer of training" technique to enable the child to master new words. Each series has its own procedures and should be evaluated in terms of sequencing of skills and its appropriateness for a particular child's needs.

An Appropriate Setting
for the Handicapped Child

During an evaluation of a local school district, some members of the state's special education team visited schools where handicapped students were said to be totally integrated. Actual classroom situations revealed a different story:

> In a health class, where students were taking a test, a member of the evaluation team noticed a student simply copying and recopying the questions. When asked about this, the teacher said the student was mentally retarded and that was what he always did during test periods. "He's quiet," she offered, "never causes any trouble."

> In another classroom, two students were at desks in the front of the room, far removed from the rest of the class. The teacher explained these students were handicapped and had different work than the rest.

In both of these cases the environment didn't fit. The boy in the health class obviously didn't have an academic program that matched his ability at all. The students in the other classroom may have had assignments geared to their level, but their integration into the classroom was nil. They weren't participating in class discussions, nor interacting with their peers. In Chapter 8, Figure 8-2 illustrates an array of educational environments which should be available for students such as these.

Individualized instruction doesn't mean a child must always work individually. Grouping according to similar needs is desirable if the group instruction is individually appropriate for each child. Small group instruction has these advantages:

1. Children often perform better when working with classmates than in a one-to-one situation with the teacher. The right amount of peer competition increases attention.
2. Children who perform the task correctly model this response for the child who does not.
3. The teacher can use group instruction to teach and reinforce appropriate group participation and social skill.

Summary

Required knowledge for the administration of special education includes information on legal help for the handicapped, vocational rehabilitation services, and what constitutes an appropriate education. Tests, texts, and the educational setting are important parts of this education.

Chapter Five

A Pocketbook of Vital Facts

A handicapped student's interest is in his future. He's going to spend the rest of his life there.

PL 94-142 specifies eleven handicapping conditions. We're giving you important facts about each one. You can refer to this information when implementing your program, talking with parents, responding to questions, and when addressing an audience.

Hearing Impaired

Three categories of hearing impairment are given in PL 94-142, *deaf, deaf-blind,* and *hard-of-hearing.* Academically, the deaf and hard-of-hearing student is potentially able to keep up with his normal-hearing classmates, with the aid of special education services that offset his impairment. The healthy deaf child can run, jump, play ball, and take part in all physical education programs his peers do. He can, and should, follow a regular school curriculum.

The degree of hearing loss alone is insufficient to determine his educational programming. A planning team must determine how he functions personally, socially, and academically; and how he responds to speech, speech signs, and other environmental sounds, both with and without a hearing aid. Variables affecting his learning are motivation, his parent's interest, community acceptance, the child's intelligence, and the severity of the hearing loss. A child with severe hearing impairment who is unable to progress in regular classes should be considered for a self-contained classroom or a special school. But make it open-ended. As soon as the student shows he can benefit from regular school placement he should be entered there.

For every hearing impaired child, these questions should be considered before integration into a regular classroom:

1. When integrated, will the student continue to receive the special services necessary for him to benefit from the non-restrictive environment?

2. Is the receiving teacher informed regarding the problems of the hearing impaired student? And is she prepared to help him learn in accordance with his handicap?

3. Are the parents in agreement with the placement in a regular classroom? Is the child?

4. Will the regular students give the hearing impaired child the consideration they expect to give and get from each other?

5. Is the regular class small enough so that the teacher can devote some time to the hearing impaired student with his special problems?

6. Is the lighting in the classroom bright enough to read lips, if this is necessary?

7. Is the child seated in the room to his best advantage?

8. Do sound films, shown in the classroom, have subtitles?

9. Are fire exits and alarm systems set up to alert the deaf?

When these questions are resolved, the hearing impaired child should progress in school at a rate consonant with his potential.

The deaf-blind child is seldom integrated into a regular class, even on a partial basis. Individual instruction, given by a flexible, intuitive teacher, seems to be most beneficial. Educational programs for these and all hearing impaired children should begin as soon as possible — ideally an infancy.

In school, a counselor who has training or experience in communicating with the deaf is a necessity. When untrained personnel have occasion to communicate with a deaf student, it is suggested that this be done with pad and pencil. Writing will reduce any guesswork and anxiety for the deaf person. Lipreading is only a partial help, as the average deaf "listener" perceives only 30%-40% of spoken English by looking at the lips of the speaker.

The hearing impaired student should be given information about his disability. This is often overlooked; yet the informed person is the best spokesman for himself and the deaf community. For information on his legal rights, the National Center for Law and the Deaf (NCLD) can be contacted at Gallaudet College, Washington D.C. 20002.

Mental Retardation

Mental retardation means significantly subaverage general intellectual functioning, existing concurrently with deficits in adaptive behavior and manifested during the developmental period, which adversely affects a child's educational performance (PL 94-142). The affliction can be caused by infection, rubella contracted by a pregnant mother, brain injury, lack of sufficient oxygen to the brain, hydrocephalus, and the chromosomal abnormality known as Down's Syndrome (mongoloidism). Care must be taken when categorizing the mentally retarded because there are so many borderline cases and cases where children appear retarded but function normally when given the proper education and environment.

To simplify educational planning, this condition is divided into four levels:

1. *Mildly Mentally Retarded* students learn basic academic skills. They benefit in the regular classroom, with the assistance of some special education in most instances. Given the proper education and training, this population functions fairly independently in society. On the Wechsler Scale the mild retardate attains an intelligence quotient between 55 and 70.

2. *Moderately Mentally Retarded* students attain very limited academic goals. They learn simple self-help, social, and occupational skills. The moderately retarded child has an IQ between 40 and 55.

3. *Severely Mentally Retarded* learn a few self-help and work skills. They require continuous and close supervision. The extrapolated intelligence quotient is between 25 and 40.

4. *Profoundly Mentally Retarded* persons require total support. Some may learn simple self-help tasks. The extrapolated intelligence is 24 and below.

In the area of diagnosis and evaluation, the American Association on Mental Deficiency (AAMD) publishes an excellent instrument, *Adaptive Behavior Scale for Evaluating the Mentally Retarded.*

Mental age, rather than chronological, is considered the criterion for initiating instruction for the retarded. However, this doesn't mean the thirteen year old should be put with second graders because he's reading on that level. Healthy social growth requires he be taught in his peer group environment.

The mentally retarded need a counselor who understands the handicap. Parent involvement is also important. Bus drivers, safety officers, volunteers, and regular teachers should be able to counsel the mentally retarded in the area in which they work with them. The National Association for Retarded Citizens, Closer Look, and the American Association on Mental Deficiency offer information on the legal rights of this group.

Multihandicapped

Multihandicapped refers to concomitant impairments, such as mentally retarded-blind, and deaf-blind (given a separate category under PL 94-142.) Multihandicapped children with severe educational problems are not integrated into regular classes, but they should participate in campus life as much as possible. Thus, the administrator of special education should consider the requirement of least restrictive environment before placements are made. Their educational programs could be placed in "Centers" located on school campuses throughout the district.

The handicapping conditions of these children are so pronounced that they usually receive help from birth. But we can't be lulled by this statement. If a child in a class for the moderately mentally retarded fails to achieve, the possibility of a concomitant handicap, such as hearing loss or severe emotional disturbance, shouldn't be overlooked. A helpful guide for persons working with the multihandicapped is titled, *How to Help Your Child — A Guide for Parents of Multiply Handicapped Children.* The first part describes a public school program, the second explains how parents can help their child at home. Write to:

> Pennsylvania Department of Special Education
> Harrisburg, Pennsylvania

Orthopedically Impaired and Other Health Impaired

Within these categories the following terms are commonly used:

1. Cerebral palsy (See Chapter 4 on Developmental Disabilities.)
2. Cystic fibrosis — an inherited disease which causes chronic infection and obstruction of the lungs.
3. Epilepsy (See Chapter 4 on Developmental Disabilities.)
4. Hydrocephalus — an abnormal increase in cerebrospinal fluid resulting in enlargement of the skull.
5. Muscular dystrophy — a chronic disease of the muscles evidenced by a gradual atrophy of the voluntary muscles.
6. Nephrosis — a degenerative condition affecting the kidneys; also known as Bright's Disease.
7. Osteomyelitis — inflammation of bone marrow and adjacent bone.
8. Rheumatic fever — believed to be caused by a strep infection. Sometimes results in damage to heart valves.
9. Rheumatoid arthritis — affects joint movement; can result in permanent joint deformities.
10. Spina bifida — a congenital condition of incomplete closure of the vertebral column, usually resulting in loss of bowel and bladder control, and loss of sensation in the lower extremities.

Usually, health impaired children are mainstreamed into regular classes. Those that require a self-contained environment are often served by a regional facility for crippled children.

Counseling should help these students become active members of the student body. Parent counseling is important because parents tend to overprotect their health impaired child. Many of them structure their lives around the child's routine. The child becomes the center of attention, which works against acceptable social interaction with other youngsters.

Seriously Emotionally Disturbed

These children exhibit one or more of the following characteristics over a long period of time and to a marked degree:

1. An inability to learn which cannot be explained by intellectual, sensory, or health factors.
2. An inability to build or maintain satisfactory relationships with peers and teachers.
3. Inappropriate behavior or feelings under normal circumstances.
4. A general pervasive mood of unhappiness or depression.
5. A tendency to develop physical symptoms or fears associated with personal or school problems.

The term doesn't include children who are socially maladjusted, unless it is determined that they are seriously emotionally disturbed.

There are a number of approaches to the treatment and education of the seriously emotionally disturbed. In some cases the instructional program is used only as a tool for the treatment; there is very little academic structure. Another approach is to treat the disturbance as a physical illness. The sociological method deals with the child in relation to the social forces surrounding him. The behaviorists use the law of reinforcement for learning, rewarding good behavior and ignoring poor.

If the school is to provide the educational setting, an environment should be established where the child knows what is expected of him. Counseling is done primarily by his specially trained teachers. Parents should be made aware of the array of services for their emotionally disturbed child.

Specific Learning Disability

Specific learning disability means a disorder in processes involved in understanding or in using language. It may manifest itself in an imperfect ability to listen, think, speak, read, write, spell, or do mathematics. The term includes such conditions as perceptual handicaps, brain injury, minimal brain dysfunction, dyslexia, and developmental aphasia. The term does not include children who have learning problems due to visual, hearing, or motor problems; mental retardation, emotional disturbance, or environmental, cultural, or economic disadvantage.

Regulations under PL 94-142 state that a multi-disciplinary team must evaluate a child suspected of having a specific learning disability. The team shall include:

1. The child's regular teacher.
2. At least one person, other than the regular teacher, qualified to conduct diagnostic examinations of children.
3. One team member, other than the regular teacher, to observe the child's academic performance in the regular classroom.

The team compiles a written report of the evaluation, which includes a statement of:

1. Whether the child has a specific learning disability and the basis for the determination.
2. The behavior noted during the observation and its relationship to the child's academic functioning.
3. Relevant medical findings.
4. Whether there is a severe discrepancy between achievement and ability.
5. The effects of any environmental, cultural, or economic disadvantage.

The team determines the child has a specific learning disability if he has a severe discrepancy between achievement and ability in one or more of these areas:

a. oral expression
b. listening comprehension
c. written expression
d. basic reading skill
e. reading comprehension
f. mathematics calculation
g. mathematics reasoning

During their school years, these children tend to be impulsive and nervous. They have a short attention span, and have problems in collecting, sorting, storing, and expressing information. They are frustrating to an uninformed teacher because the lack of achievement appears inexplicable. Yet, given an appropriate education and the correct environment they may be expected to ultimately achieve as normal adults. PL 94-142 started out by putting a 2 percent cap on the numbers of learning disabled reported by SEAs for funding purposes. The cap is now removed, as many states reported they had several times that number.

Trained counselors are important for the learning disabled. Teachers should have information about the child's evaluation, medication he may be taking, and any other special instructions. For parents there is an exemplary pamphlet prepared by the National Association for Children with Learning Disabilities. It's titled, *What Every Parent Should Know About Learning Disabilities.* Write to:

National Association for Children
with Learning Disabilities
5225 Grace St.
Pittsburgh, PA 15236

Speech Impaired

Early intervention, at about 8 years of age, is believed to aid significantly in the remediation of this problem. Students with a severe impairment in the use of words (aphasia) require extensive services. They may need a self-contained classroom, at least temporarily.

Speech pathologists list these factors — in order of importance — as contributing to success of therapy:

Elementary Level	*Secondary Level*
1. Consistent attendance	1. Student's Motivation
2. Motivation	2. Consistent attendance
3. Parent cooperation	3. Attitude of others as seen by student
4. Clinician's interest	4. Clinician's interest

Because speech impaired children often feel isolated and different from their peers, especially older students when their disability persists, counseling is needed.

Visually Handicapped

Visually handicapped includes both partially seeing and blind children under PL 94-142. Legally blind children have visual acuity for distance vision of 20/200 or less, in the better eye with best correction; or a field of vision no greater than 20 degrees.

The goal of most visually impaired students is integration into normal society; therefore, they should be educated with regular students wherever feasible. A national free hotline on information for the visually impaired is available. Call 800-424-9770. The American Foundation for the Blind (15 West 16th Street, New York, NY 10011) publishes a directory of service agencies. They also are a resource for legal rights for the blind.

Parents need support in accepting their child's disability, overcoming misconceptions about visual impairments, becoming informed about realistic limitations of the impairment, and planning an appropriate education for their child. Visually impaired students should be counseled to engage in a variety of concrete experiences, such as school plays, musical productions, sports, debates, and dances. Counselors need to be on the lookout that the visually impaired are active members of the student body.

Summary

The more you and your staff know about handicapping conditions, the greater the help you can give students and their families. PL 94-142 lists eleven types of handicap. Knowledge of these categories, and informational resources pertaining to them, is an invaluable asset for the administrator of special education.

Chapter Six

Major Points in Developing
A Special Education Staff

"Appreciation for good work" was rated eighth out of ten by supervisors, but first out of ten by workers (Job Condition Study by American Management Association).

A good special education team won't just happen, anymore than a dictionary will fall into place from an explosion in a printing factory. The ingredients are there, but without proper placement they will be of little use for the overall purpose of the undertaking. Colleges turn out trained individuals, but it's up to the special education administrator to see that each member of his staff fulfills specific needs. A person sets a high goal for himself as he tackles this job. The purpose of this chapter is to guide the administrator in achieving this end.

How to Pick Good People

It's necessary to know how to recruit good educators, utilize their capabilities, and work with them as they become strong, contributing members of the educational team. We suggest you start by preparing a separate list of the qualifications needed for each special education job you seek to fill. Include such items as the educational background required, the type of certification needed, how much experience is desired, and in what areas. When you're satisfied with this list your next step is to compile a description of the things the new person will do on the job. Here is a sample of what we mean:

Job Description for High School Teacher/Work-Experience Coordinator for the Mentally Retarded

Besides carrying the major instructional role for the mentally retarded students assigned to her class, the high school teacher/work-experience coordinator shall carry out the following activities regarding work experience:

1. Be a contributing member of the Individualized Education Program (IEP) committee required under PL 94-142.

2. Evaluate the individual vocational potential of each mentally retarded high school student.

3. Utilize the evaluation results in working with the Individualized Education Program committee.

4. Explore the community and school for vocational opportunities that are appropriate for high school mentally retarded students.

5. Contact employers who are interested in cooperating in the training of mentally retarded students.

6. Do on-site task analysis of jobs which mentally retarded students can learn.

7. Supervise students on work experience and relate their on-the-job training situations to the classroom instructional program.

8. Guide students who are in their last period, or year, of high school into paid employment.

9. Counsel with students and parents about the work-experience program.

10. Acquire knowledge about services offered by the local Division of Vocational Rehabilitation and the State Employment Office, and make referrals of students when appropriate.

11. Present public relations programs and talks to community organizations, such as Rotary Club and Lions Club, to interest them in providing work-experience opportunities and ultimate employment for the mentally retarded.

12. Utilize vocational programs such as the Neighborhood Youth Corps, and the National Association for Retarded Citizens' On-the-Job Training Program.

13. Keep informed about activities and decisions which affect the special education work-study program, such as wage and hour regulations, insurance coverage, and labor union stipulations.

The above description includes every important task pertaining to the position without becoming enmeshed in detail. You can use similar job descriptions as you interview applicants, and again when you meet during the year to evaluate the new employee's performance. Good, clear job descriptions are valuable tools of your trade.

In a large district the personnel office may handle the writing up of the job description. However, input from the special education administrator will be appreciated. Observe the chain-of-command rule, but see that your School Board knows what qualifications are needed in a teacher to fill a specific opening.

Having identified the qualifications for the job, the next step is to advertise widely.

Tips on Recruiting

There are many recruitment sources; for example, your own staff members. Let them help you find a new teacher. Good teachers often have friends with similar capabilities. A file on possible applicants is a good thing to keep up. In addition, pay attention to special education publications. Job-seekers place announcements in periodicals such as the Council for Exceptional Children publication. Also, consider the idea of placing your own advertisement for a new teacher. This can pay off if you compose good copy.

For example, if your district is in the hinterlands, write the ad so that the remote location becomes an enticement rather than a hindrance. "Get away from the city's mad rush. Come teach in central Oregon's magnificent pine woods country where Indian summer lasts until the ski snows fall." For an ad opener this should interest many job-seekers, especially creative people who seek new experiences. Get many persons to apply. Take the time you need to do it. The mistake of hiring a poor teacher costs far more than time spent on finding a good one.

A major factor when filling a position is the search of qualified minorities and handicapped persons. Your State Department of Education and the Affirmative Action Section in your State Governor's Office offer assistance with the legal aspects of this undertaking. Fair employment practices are a must.

Many districts have a policy of evaluating written applications and selecting the top four or five for personal interviews. Where an excellent applicant lives a great distance from the district, telephone calls and further written interchange may substitute. But where at all possible, the contract should be signed only after an applicant has had an on-site interview.

Key Elements in the Initial Interview

A special education administrator's human relations skill is an important part of the first interview. One of the applicants will be hired, and the direction of the partnership you and the new employee form is set at this meeting.

The interview should be private. Set a relaxed atmosphere and take as much time as needed. The application information will guide the discussion. Questions that elicit how the person will fulfill requirements under PL 94-142 are important. For example; the philosophy of educating the handicapped in the least restrictive environment necessitates that the special teacher work in close harmony with regular staff members. Does the applicant see this as part of her job?

Another point to discuss is the stress PL 94-142 puts on inservice. Before a teacher is hired she should be aware of the fact that taking inservice courses is required.

The applicant should be impressed with the seriousness with which your district takes the job she's applying for. Teachers aspire to do a fine job, but if they perceive their aspirations are higher than those of the prospective employer, they may lower their sights. There's a principle which states that on a job a person rises to the level of his incompetency. Be sure this level isn't reached by your staff before it's necessary. Select strong, resilient teachers to begin with, and set high but attainable goals for them to achieve.

How to Make the Most of Your Present Staff

Don't leave teachers in situations where they are frustrated. Good teachers either quit or become mediocre when they see no way out of an assignment which undermines their efforts. A district policy of lateral transfers can help these situations. One teacher's dilemma can be a stimulating assignment for another, and both may be fine educators. The policy and rationale of lateral transfers is a point to make during the pre-hire interview.

Lateral transfers of students also works:

> Recently, a supervisor was threatened with two lawsuits. One by a parent if his disruptive child wasn't allowed to remain in a program for the educable mentally retarded; and another by the teacher if the supervisor didn't take action to remove the child. Fortunately, the parent agreed to a transfer to another school, and a teacher in a similar program across town accepted the challenge to work with the youngster. It all turned out very well.

Observe each of your teachers; you'll notice that those who are basically weak don't become stronger when placed, or left, in difficult positions. If you must keep them on your staff, transfer them to easier situations.

Putting Dynamism in Special Education Inservice Programs

We now turn to the task of maintaining or improving your teachers' skills — and to the goal of training your staff in procedures required under PL 94-142. Dynamic inservice courses go a long way toward attainment of these ends. Keep the following in mind as you plan your professional growth programs:

1. Public Law 94-142 necessitates two kinds of inservice; one informs teachers about the law, the other trains them in implementing the law's requirements.

2. A resource for inservice courses is your State Educational Agency. Under the regulations of PL 94-142 your SEA can be called on to:

   a. Initiate innovative and experimental inservice programs related to implementing the law.

   b. Conduct an annual needs assessment of new and re-trained personnel.

   c. Insure that inservice is available to all personnel engaged in the education of the handicapped.

   d. Include in their inservice programs participation incentives such as released time for attendance, payment for participation and per diem expenses, and granting of credit.

e.   Involve local staff in presenting inservice programs.

3. Provide topnotch instructors who can transmit know-how in the shortest possible time. A poor inservice course results in justified dissatisfaction among teachers.

An example of a delivery method teachers like is the modified Delphi approach:

Let us say a district plans to give inservice to regular and special teachers regarding the requirement of least restrictive environment. In essence: The instructor explains what is meant by least restrictive environment, then the class is divided into groups with one person in each group acting as facilitator. The groups generate issues involved with the implementation of this requirement. They write them down, prioritize them, and share them with the class. Following this, the groups reconvene and dig out the problems embodied in the issues. Solutions to the problems are sought and forces operating for and against the solutions are brought forth and examined. They're noted down and also presented to the whole class for discussion.

This involves much audience interaction and results in a rich interchange of information between regular and special educators. Teachers enjoy this type of course. Straight lecture-type presentations should be discouraged.

Tips on Training Classroom Aides

In a special education program run by a hardworking administrator, it was obvious the teachers weren't utilizing the aide money he'd budgeted for them. When asked why, they replied it took so much time to work out a training program and train an aide that it just wasn't worth it. He went to work on the problem and after some research came up with a first draft of a training package for classroom aides.

Next, he and one of his teachers who was using an aide went over his procedures, and after some changes this teacher became the first trainer of resource room aides. Other teachers were invited to observe the trainer whenever their schedules permitted, or released time could be arranged for them. The administrator was active in the first training sessions, but his participation isn't necessary anymore. Enough teachers have experience in training aides to help out any new staff member. Initially developed for volunteers, it is now used for paid aides as well. Experienced aides, new to the district, go through the same training, but in a shorter length of time. Here's the district's training routine:

1. To recruit they survey the community and check with school counselors, principals, volunteer agencies, parent groups, social groups, and college service organizations.

2. The volunteer aides are generally selected from high schools and colleges. Paid aides are older: they must be high school graduates. Some hold teaching certificates and, in this day of teacher overload, take the job as an entry into the profession.

3. Applicants are screened and interviewed by the resource room teacher, and at times by the building principal. The experience the applicant has had with children and the amount of time she has to offer are selection factors. A commitment of three hours a week minimum is required.

4. For high school volunteers it is beneficial to draw up a student-aide contract of commitment responsibilities. This is approved and signed by the applicant, her parents, the school counselor, and the resource room teacher. Where appropriate, school credit is given.

5. When applicants are accepted, an orientation lecture is given by a resource room teacher.

The talk follows this outline:

AIDE-IN-TRAINING-LECTURE

I. Defining the resource room:
   a. An instructional setting to which a student comes for specially designed instruction as prescribed in his IEP.
   b. The resource room teacher provides instructional support to both the student and his regular teacher.
   c. A student usually attends the resource room on a part time basis. His time in regular classrooms is increased whenever feasible.

II. Type of student eligible for service:

    a. The room admits students eligible for special education as defined in PL 94-142:

        1. Mentally Retarded
        2. Learning Disabled
        3. Seriously Emotionally Disturbed
        4. Orthopedically Impaired or Other Health Impaired
        5. Multihandicapped (combinations of the above disabilities)

    b. Students are served on a first-come, first-served basis, with the following priorities:

        1. Most severely handicapped
        2. Primary students (in elementary schools)
        3. Other eligible students as space and time permit

III. Referral:

    a. A referral results from the development of a student's individualized education program.

    b. (Special education referral procedures are presented here if appropriate. See Chapter 11 for details.)

IV. Scheduling the resource room student in the school setting:

    a. A student new to the school is assigned to a regular classroom on the basis of his age and current academic and social functioning.

    b. The principal makes the final decision regarding the regular classroom placement of a student.

    c. Resource room teacher and regular teacher establish a schedule for the student, with the consensus of other IEP team members.

    d. Resource room teacher sets up a program for the new student based on written goals set at the student's IEP meeting.

V. Physical organization of resource room:

    a. It is located near the center of the building for easy access to all classrooms.

    b. The room is divided as follows:

        1. Independent seatwork area
        2. Small group-teaching stations

3. Free time area consisting of instructional games area and a reading corner

VI. Staff jobs in resource room:

   a. Direct teaching of individuals and small groups.
   b. Implementing behavior management and other programs specified by the IEP.
   c. Floor managing, which is supervision of the independent seatwork and free time areas. A uniform signaling device is used by students needing help.

VII. Behavior required of trainee:

   a. Information pertaining to students is not to be discussed outside the room.
   b. The principal is to be involved in all decisions pertaining to school operation and staff.
   c. Cooperation with other school staff is essential.

Following this introductory lecture the trainee observes in the resource room for a minimum of an hour. A pre-test is then given. It's designed to inform the resource teacher about the applicant's knowledge of classroom procedures, and to provide evidence of the trainee's growth when the same test is given at post-test time. This pre/post-test consists of situational multiple-choice questions:

PRE/POST TEST

Directions: Circle the correct letter, or letters, that best answer each question.

1. You are working with a child and he doesn't respond to your request to start working. You should:

   a. Notify resource room teacher
   b. Remind him that the work must be finished before any other activity can begin
   c. Demand that he work or else
   d. Squeeze his arm till he works

2. A student hits you for some reason. You should:

   a. Pretend you are really hurt
   b. Hit the student back immediately
   c. Ignore it
   d. Inform the teacher immediately

3. In working with a group, one child starts bothering another child. You should:

   a. Give praise to those who are working or attending
   b. Tell him to knock it off
   c. Ignore the behavior and do nothing
   d. Place him in time-out

4. A child needs help on a word or problem. When he gives the correct answer, you should:

   a. Count it as an error when recording
   b. Count it correct when recording
   c. Don't count it
   d. Give him a second chance

5. When a child has read 5 "Say Sounds" wrong and 32 right, you should record in which of the following ways:

   a. 5/32
   b. 27
   c. 32/5
   d. 32 correct/5 errors

6. The classroom teacher is working with a child, and you need an answer to a minor question. You should:

   a. Get the teacher's attention by saying her name
   b. Get the teacher's attention by standing near her
   c. Wait for a break

7. A child is punished by being put behind a screen. He starts popping up from behind the screen. If the teacher is busy, you should:

   a. Ignore the child
   b. Tell him to be quiet right now
   c. Praise those children who are quiet
   d. Tell the class not to look at this student

8. You are the floor manager while the teacher is working with small groups. A child is having

trouble with an assignment. When you try to help him he says he wants the other teacher. You should:

    a. Ask the teacher for help
    b. Tell the child not to argue
    c. Force the child to do it your way
    d. Tell the child while you are working with him, you are the teacher

9. As you walk into the room a student talks out to you with a statement or a question. You should:

    a. Place him in time-out
    b. Say good morning and answer the question
    c. Indicate you heard him, but let him know you can't respond
    d. Ignore him

10. A child completes a math assignment with 50% errors. The first thing you should do is:

    a. Tell the child to do the page over
    b. Check the errors with red checks and have the child correct them
    c. Say "Wow, you really did a good job "
    d. Focus on all the correct ones then point out the errors for correction

11. A student asks you a question that you do not know the answer to. You should:

    a. Make up an answer so you won't look bad
    b. Tell the student it is not an important point and go on
    c. Ignore the question
    d. Admit you don't know and search out the answer

12. You are sick and can't go to class. You should:

    a. Not go, and tell the teacher the next time you are there
    b. Go anyway because you have work to do
    c. Call in, so the teacher will not plan for you
    d. None of the above

13. All you ever do is run dittos and staple. You're bored and want to do something else. You should:

    a. Quit
    b. Ask for a transfer to another resource room
    c. Do poor work
    d. Discuss your feeling with the teacher

Following the taking of this test, the trainee is given material to read pertaining to the teaching of all children, handicapped or not. The material depends on the individual trainee and the class she is being trained for. Articles on "How to Take the Put-Downs Out of Praise," and how to say "You've Done Very Well in a Variety of Ways," are fine for all trainees. Meanwhile, the trainee observes individual and group teaching, especially in the areas of reading and math.

The next step is one of observation, also — only this time the trainee has a teacher-observation form to follow (Figure 6-1). The form has three sections: 1) The cues given by the teacher. Are they appropriate or not? 2) The consequences of the student's response as handled by the teacher. Is the teacher's response appropriate? Does she fail to give feedback? 3) The comments written down by the observer.

The trainee will utilize this form a number of times during her training period. When she reaches the point where she instructs children, the trainer will utilize it to check off her observations of the trainee's behavior. Since much of the recording done on the form is by personal judgment, the person observed and the observer always go over the form together after its completion.

When the trainee uses the observation form in a reliable fashion, she is given the pre-test a second time. A score of 90% right on the test indicates she is ready to do some instruction. This requires preparation: She reads the program of the child she is to instruct, and the long and short term goals in the area of instruction. She collects all necessary supplies and equipment. While the trainee is instructing, the trainer utilizes the observation form. Later, she discusses it with the trainee. The trainer models again, at trainee's request. The same post-observation procedure takes place.

After the trainee is able to instruct individuals and small groups, she is trained as a floor manager. That is, she is taught how to supervise children who are working independently at their desks or at the free time area. To begin with, the trainee becomes familiar with the seatwork the students have been assigned to do. She then observes the teacher, using the teacher observation form until she feels comfortable with the knowledge she has acquired. When the trainee acts as floor manager, the teacher utilizes the observation form. The teacher alternately models floor management and observes the trainee's progress in this area until the trainee can take charge on her own.

How to Have First-Rate Staff Meetings

Your staff meetings will confirm your leadership. That is if they are handled right:

1. In September, inform your staff of the time and place of the meetings for the year.
2. Write up an agenda before each meeting and give a copy to every teacher and to your supervisor.
3. Always start and end the meeting on time.
4. Make it a point to confer with a teacher who has been absent from a meeting. Let her know how important her attendance is.
5. Serve refreshments, even if you have to have a "contribution plate" on the coffee table.
6. The informality of a coffee hour helps teachers unwind — and sometimes unload the troubles that have occurred between meetings. Listen to what they say and make mental notes of pertinent information to follow up on later.
7. Be the leader of the meeting. If you take your leadership seriously, your staff will also. Joke and laugh with your people but remain aware that the responsibility for making the meeting count remains with you.
8. Consider ideas such as these for interesting meetings:
   a. Teachers share ideas, at one meeting at least.
   b. Regular teachers talk about the handicapped in the regular room.
   c. Outside experts demonstrate their expertise. (Educational materials salesmen give interesting presentations. On swings through the area they will visit remote districts if given lead time.)

Figure 6-1
TEACHER OBSERVATION FORM

Teacher _____

Situation _____

School _____

Observer _____

Date _____

Time _____ to _____

Intervals of 5 minutes	Number of children observed	Number of children on task	1. CUES GIVEN BY TEACHER	
			Appr. (Ex. "When I touch it, you say it.")	Not appr. (Ex. "Do what I do.")

2. TEACHER'S RESPONSE TO STUDENT PERFORMANCE

Appr. (Ex. "Right, it is a magnet." or "No, it is not a magnet.")	Not appr. (Too much praise. Too little.)	No feedback at all

3. OBSERVER'S COMMENTS

87

Summary

In building a good staff, an administrator has written descriptions of his district's special education jobs, and he knows how to recruit for these positions. He places teachers in the right spots and provides for the training of volunteers and other aides. To maintain and improve his staff, he makes available exemplary inservice courses, and holds worthwhile staff meetings.

Chapter Seven

Providing Assistance to Your Teaching Staff

Staunchly resist the compulsive feeling that plagues many administrators...that they need to have the answers to all problems. Ask your staff for their alternatives, opinions, and recommendations.

The law can insure that the education is free, and that an education programming team will develop a planned curriculum for a child. But it's the teacher who imparts this curriculum to the student. The assistance which you provide for a teacher is one of the most important contributions you can make for handicapped students.

Helping Teachers Teach by Objectives

One of the refinements of present day education is the art of teaching by objectives. Yet there are some teachers who still don't use this valuable tool. Our examples illustrate this point:

1. Student A comes to his reading group:
   a. He's not aware of any objectives set for him.
   b. His teacher sees her role as simply correcting his errors.
   c. There is no chart to measure his progress.
2. Student B comes to his reading group:
   a. His specific objective is learning to read big words by separating them into small ones.

    b. He has practiced this with familiar words such as Sunday and bookbag.

    c. He understands the chart that measures his progress.

    d. He's eager to meet this new challenge.

The teacher of Student A is spending as much of her pupil's time in reading as the second teacher, but it's in a hit-and-miss fashion. She needs to learn to teach by objectives. The inservice course is a way to provide this assistance:

1. Orangize an inservice on setting instructional goals for all your teachers. This will include those who need extensive help without singling out particular persons.

2. Develop the course to insure much staff participation and sharing so all will profit.

3. Hire a teacher, perhaps one of your staff, who is trained in teaching by objectives, to give the course.

4. Or contact the special education division of your SEA and tell them your district needs. (To provide for personnel development is a requirement for SEAs under PL 94-142.)

Items of information you will want teachers to acquire during this inservice are:

1. Instructional objectives describe specific learning sequences within a course or unit of study.

2. Objectives should be stated in behavioral outcome language such as "student will know," if the acquisition of knowledge is the objective; or "student will be able to," if a particular process is the objective; or "student will value," if value is the objective.

3. Instructional objectives are part of a larger curriculum scheme described by course goals. Course goals are also defined as learner outcome statements, but on a broader scale. They provide the foundation for the individualized instructional objectives.

4. The following are examples of instructional objectives for low-potential students in a math class. A performance indicator (PI) is given with each objective.

a. Student will be able to match geometric shapes.

PI: When given two sets of cards having the same geometric shapes, the student matches like cards from each set.

b. Student will be able to find geometric shapes.

PI: When presented with a mixed group of shapes and asked to find a named shape (circle, triangle), the student selects the correct shape.

c. Student will be able to name geometric shapes.

PI: When presented with a series of geometric shapes (circle, triangle, square), the student names each shape correctly.

Teachers in an inservice who learn to state behavioral objectives in a clear, concise manner will consider the time well spent. However, the inservice course isn't always necessary. The administrator of special education who is knowledgeable in the area of behavioral objectives, and has the time, may want to meet individually with teachers and work out ways together for the teacher to develop this skill.

Hints for Helping the Resource Room Teacher

In a district where schools are left pretty much on their own as far as implementing their programs, a visitor made this observation: School "A" had the expected special education components — a resource room with an aide where children with varying handicapping conditions came for special instruction. Both teacher and aide taught full time.

The educational resource center in School "B" presented a different picture. The question, "Who is the teacher in here?" was answered by a capable looking woman. "I'm the teacher/manager, if that's what you mean," she said. Then she pointed to four other persons working with small groups or individuals. "There are a number of teachers here, as you can see."

Because of the complexity of modern day special education, resource room teachers are beginning to see themselves as room managers who plan and oversee the delivery of programs, rather than doing everything themselves. Basic to the assistance you can give these teachers, is an understanding of what this new role entails. In Chapter 6 we described a resource room in the section titled "Tips on Training Classroom Aides." Here are some aspects of the teacher/manager role:

1. Teachers in special education resource rooms are becoming less and less identified with particular areas of exceptionality. They provide programs based on individual pupil needs, instead of carrying out a traditional, set curriculum for a child because he is mentally retarded, or learning disabled, for example.

2. The jobs of the resource teacher/manager include:
   a. Laying out instructional tasks. This is often in the form of work packets for room aides.
   b. Providing materials, media, and evaluation procedures to be used.
   c. Seeing that someone — herself, an aide, a volunteer, — does the instruction.
   d. Monitoring the instruction.
   e. Keeping records.

3. Additional tasks of the resource room teacher:
   a. Participate in IEP meetings.
   b. Work with regular teachers.
   c. Confer with parents.
   d. Train room aides. (Described in Chapter 6.)

The resource room is committed to:

1. Mainstreaming. All children spend part of the day in a regular classroom, starting the day there for roll call, lunch, and announcements.

2. Service across handicapping areas. The instruction pertains to a child's education, rather than to his handicapping condition.

3. Prescriptive programming. A child enters the resource room with a set of short and long term goals.

4. Monitoring daily performance. When a student meets the pre-set criteria that show he has obtained a goal, or a step toward a goal, he advances to the next step. If he demonstrates he is failing to advance, alternate methods of instruc-

tion are adopted. This insures that the child isn't taught in a repetitive fashion day after day, when he clearly isn't making progress.

Because of the large amount of duplication, the resource room has its own supply of duplicating masters and paper, as well as pencils, felt tip pens, and other classroom supplies. Audio-visual equipment includes media such as a Language Master, a cassette recorder and cassettes, a record player and headphones, and an overhead projector. Examples of teacher-made items are progress charts, and flags for signaling need for teacher help.

Guidelines for Helpful Supervision

The administrator of special education is in a double role if he both administers and supervises. Administration is considered to be the organization and operation of programs, while supervision deals with the improvement of instruction. Here, we're assuming you're combining these functions.

Today's teachers are well trained and want to do a good job. They'll respond to a supervisory program that includes their participation. So, before making classroom visits a well-organized supervisor does a number of pre-observation tasks:

1. Review the job description with the teacher to assure both himself and the teacher that her duties and responsibilities are understood.
2. Inform the teacher of his method of supervision. He may set a date and time for visitations, or he may visit her room sometime during a certain week — no set hour. (One supervisor sets aside parts of three months, October, January, and April, to do his observations. The month just following each of these is used to write up evaluations. In May, which follows the last observation month of the school year, the final evaluations are completed.)
3. Inform the teacher that he will always follow up his visit with a conference. (Never pay a visit to a classroom without some feedback.)
4. Talk over with the teacher what they both can expect her to accomplish. The list of jobs might go like this:

a. Insure that long and short term objectives are stated in the students' IEPs.

b. Have lesson plans that aid students to meet these objectives.

c. Consider individual student learning modalities and abilities when planning and implementing instruction.

d. Provide frequent and prompt feedback.

e. Utilize media and materials appropriate for the individual child.

f. Exhibit positive verbal and non-verbal influence on children.

g. Show respect for students.

h. Encourage each individual to express ideas and feelings clearly.

i. Use techniques and materials that are stimulating to students who have differing abilities and interests.

j. Explain goals and procedures for evaluation to students where appropriate. Develop these with students when practical.

k. Be consistent with disciplinary procedures.

l. Provide an atmosphere in which students remain at task.

m. When the need arises, refer students to appropriate support services; e.g., nurse, counselor, community service agency.

n. Exercise appropriate care for the safety of students.

o. Encourage positive self-image in students.

p. Make appropriate and efficient use of paraprofessionals.

q. Use prompt and accurate communication with parents concerning their child's progress and behavior.

r. Incorporate innovative teaching derived from educational research and demonstration.

s. Keep records on students' progress.

t. Confer with regular teachers and other school staff who are involved in the students' programs. Utilize their input.

During follow-up conferences the supervisor reviews his observations with the teacher. If there are areas that need improvement, he and the teacher select one or more at a time to work on.

Our next section presents ways to formally summarize your observations and work with the incompetent teacher.

Tips on Overcoming Teaching Incompetencies

You have observed a teacher enough to be able to document where help is needed. The teacher and you have gone over the list of expected accomplishments presented in the last section. You also have discussed those sections in Chapter 10 titled "Characteristics of Good Classroom Teachers for All Children," and "Special Classroom Requirements for the Handicapped." Items you both will work on to improve her teaching have been selected.

To help set this up in a business-like manner, the worksheet in Figure 7-1 is suggested. It can be used as is, or modified to suit your circumstances. In any case, you should employ some instrument that puts the documentation of needed instructional improvement in the hands of the teacher, and on a formal basis. Experience has shown that unless objectives for improvement are written down and acknowledged by both the teacher and supervisor, little or no change takes place.

After the improvement worksheet is filled out, you will want to follow up with more observations. It may help to employ the form given in Figure 7-2. It is a formal worksheet which both you and the teacher can fill out separately after an observation period. During the follow-up conference, compare your write-up with the teacher's and discuss items where continued improvement is necessary. This worksheet can be used for all classroom visitations if it suits your needs.

For the most part, the inadequacies in teaching methods will be taken care of by the foregoing procedures. But perhaps you have a teacher who is not making the necessary improvement. More serious steps must be undertaken. Again, we resort to a written document. In filling out the form in Figure 7-3, the tone and language should reflect a feeling of growth, improvement, and continuity of effort.

Along with the notice in Figure 7-3, you may want to use the memo in Figure 7-4. Note that copies of both forms are put in the employee's file, and that the district superintendent signs the Memo.

Figure 7-1
PERFORMANCE IMPROVEMENT
WORKSHEET

Teacher: _____ Supervisor: _____

Date: _____

Improvement of instruction is the main purpose of the teacher evaluation process. Areas for improvement may be gained from feedback after classroom observations by your supervisor, or by your own insight into your teaching content and methods. Read the following questions, talk them over with your supervisor if you wish, and answer them in the space below.

1. What desired change do you want to achieve? (Identify performance to be acquired.)
2. What action will you take? (Specify conditions under which the change will be made.)
3. What resources will you need? (Examples are time, materials, training, and supervision.)
4. What indicators will you use to assess achievement of the change?
5. When should the change be completed? (Timeline)

1. Change desired: _____

2. Action: _____

3. Resources needed: _____

4. Indicators: _____

5. Timeline: _____

Figure 7-2
FORMAL OBSERVATION
WORKSHEET

Teacher _____ Supervisor _____

Date of Visit _____ Subject Taught _____

Time of Visit _____

1. Objective(s) of the lesson:

2. Lesson plans, procedure(s):

3. Teacher's (or Supervisor's) evaluation of learner outcome:

4. Specifically, this observation noted the following (e.g., skills, techniques, pupil interaction):

5. Other information pertinent to instructional procedures:

Figure 7-3
NOTICE OF PLAN
FOR PROFESSIONAL
IMPROVEMENT

Name _____ Employe Status _____

Assignment _____ School _____ Date _____

1. It has been determined that the above employe's professional performance needs special attention and assistance. Both the teacher and supervisor perceive this need. The following presents an assessment of the performance and a plan to overcome the weaknesses in it.

    a. Skills and knowledge which are found to need improvement are based upon these observations:

    b. The skills and knowledge which need attention at this time are:

2. The plan designed to bring about this improvement includes (e.g., district professional growth program, inservice courses, background reading, and conference with the teacher's supervisor):

3. The above will be accomplished, or noticeable improvement achieved, on or before _____, by which time we will have a review conference. We may at that time agree that improvement is satisfactory, or we may wish to set revised or new performance goals leading to further improvement.

_____   _____
Employe's Signature   Supervisor's Signature

(Indicates the report has been read and discussed.)

                                    Date _____

copies: Employe, Supervisor, Employe's File, Personnel Director

Figure 7-4
MEMO ABOUT
EVALUATION STATUS

Main School District #1
Maintown, U.S.A. 03030

Date: _____

NOTICE: EVALUATION STATUS

TO: _____   _____
     Employe's Name   Employe's Status

FROM: _____
     Name and Title

This is to advise you that from this date to the completion of your employment, or until another conclusion is reached, the district evaluation procedures will no longer be used solely for the improvement of your services to the district, but also for obtaining and recording information about your continued employment by the district.

Please sign your name here as indication that you have received this document, a copy of which is attached for your use.

_____

                         Employe's Signature

_____

                        Supervisor's Signature

_____

                 Signature of School
             District Superintendent

copies: Employe, Supervisor, Employe's file, Personnel Director

Through all of this, you continue to work with the teacher as long as there is sufficient improvement to warrant your time.

Hints on Terminating Employment

When everything possible has been done and there still isn't significant improvement, the decision is made to terminate the teacher's employment. This is time consuming but should not be considered impossible. Two examples illustrate this point:

> An administrator of special education, wanting to terminate an incompetent teacher, visited the classroom often and recorded his observations. He noticed in particular that the teacher marked A's and 100's on papers that had errors and demonstrated incorrect procedures for arriving at answers. He gathered up these papers and discussed them with the teacher. The teacher didn't change, the supervisor continued to gather papers, and when the showdown came this evidence was the clincher in getting the teacher relieved of her duties. The teacher then approached the powerful NEA Chapter in her state to go to bat for her, but they took one look at the sheaf of papers the supervisor had collected and said there was nothing they could do against evidence like that.

Another administrator of special education employs this system:

> A person suspected of being incompetent has two evaluations. The first one is completed in late fall. The specific areas of poor performance and incompetence are written up and discussed with the teacher. If the performance does not come up to the satisfactory level by the spring evaluation, the teacher receives a notice of non-renewal of contract no later than the middle of May. About 10 percent of those fired have taken their case to court. None were successful in being reinstated. The evaluations were too well documented.

Let's summarize the points these examples illustrate. When considering a termination:

1. Continue to communicate with the teacher.
2. Keep all observation records and previous evaluation.
3. Gather on-site data which demonstrate incompetent teaching and teaching content. (We've mentioned improper grad-

ing of papers. Other examples are showing inappropriate films habitually, and failure to follow a student's IEP.)

4. Have everything in writing. Date all material.
5. Don't compile data on unorthodox activities during a teacher's off-school hours. Civil liberties groups, lawyers, and even the teacher's union can argue that this doesn't pertain.
6. Give systematic advance notice of non-renewal of contract.

Guidelines for Purchase and Care of Materials and Equipment

A recent survey indicates that 95 percent of classroom presentations are made with some form of instructional aid, yet only about 3 percent of school budgets are allocated for these items. The need for careful selection and use of educational media and supplies is apparent.

Districts handle the buying and using of equipment in various ways. Procedures proven to be efficient are described as follows:

1. The administrator of special education sets up procedures for purchase and care of materials and equipment.
2. He gives teachers the procedural information and sees they are informed about commercial teaching aids in their field.
3. Each teacher is budgeted an amount of money for materials and small equipment. (Materials are considered consumable items; equipment can be used over and over.)
4. Large items such as stoves, kilns, audio-visual equipment, and special physical education apparatus are purchased through the district and distributed to classrooms as needed.
5. The repair of special education equipment goes through the regular school channels that process the care of all equipment in the building.
6. All equipment and materials provided for regular students are available to special students as well. Handicapped students have equal access to the school's media resource center.
7. Careful buying is imperative. For hints on this, see "Pointers on Budgeting," in Chapter 1.

How Conferences and Workshops
Help Special Educators

Once an administrator of special education who, a number of years previously, had moved from a rural community to a large city district was asked what some of the major differences were between the two localities. "Well," he said, "I've noticed that special education teachers in large cities don't change jobs as often as teachers in small districts do. And I think I know at least one reason why."

To the obvious "Why do they?" he responded, "Special ed teachers in districts far removed from one another don't have a chance to talk with other special teachers about their problems and successes. They feel isolated and so move on to where they hope there will be more of a chance for interchange of ideas. An unfortunate situation, because it's difficult to build a solid special education program when personnel is constantly changing."

This story illustrates one of the reasons why teachers should go to conferences. Especially teachers in remote localities. Let's itemize the reasons:

1. The conference, or workshop, provides the opportunity for renewal of enthusiasm and the professional exchange that teachers need.

2. Released time for professional meetings encourages good teachers to remain in a district.

3. Good teachers are attracted to districts that arrange for teachers to attend conferences and other professional meetings.

4. Teachers share what they learn at conferences with their colleagues. Thus, the whole district benefits.

Summary

Helping teachers teach by objectives is an important task for the administrator of special education. Teachers also need assistance in setting up and managing a resource room; the proper educational equipment and materials are essential. Of major importance to the administrator are procedures for a helpful evaluation of his staff. Workshops and conferences provide the shot-in-the-arm we all need from time to time.

Chapter Eight

Guidelines for Applying PL 94-142 to the Regular District Program

Poor communication was identified as the most significant barrier to achieving excellence by managers of 198 companies in three countries.

Jean Piaget, the great Swiss psychologist, once remarked that intelligence is demonstrated in three ways. The lowest form is manifested by individuals unable to adapt to normal changes in the environment. The environment must be changed by others if the survival needs of this group are to be met. The second level is made up of individuals who adapt normally to their environment. The third and highest form is manifested by those who not only adapt to their environment, but can also change it to suit their needs and the needs of others.

The administrator of special education has to be in this last group. He has to recast the lagging environment in order that changes mandated by PL 94-142 can be implemented. You start doing this at the top echelon.

Explaining PL 94-142 to District Officials

Public Law 94-142 cannot be explained in a catch-as-catch-can manner. It is too extensive, too revolutionary, and at this initial period in its history too difficult to be intellectually absorbed quickly. Although signed into law in 1975, PL 94-142 is still in the process of being implemented, in full or in part, in many districts. It's your job to provide input as its implementation goes forward.

One way to do this is to ask for time at administrative level meetings to inform and up-date your colleagues. Handle this time well:

1. Take cognizance of where your colleagues are regarding PL 94-142. It's self-defeating to start updating on information about which your audience has sketchy, if any, basic facts.

2. Cover a certain amount of ground at one meeting. Make a few statements, then elicit responses in order to clear up any misinterpretation of what you have said.

3. Address those items in PL 94-142 pertinent to situations which involve the administrators who are in your audience.

4. Keep in mind that you probably will be telling the regular school administrators more than they want to hear. They'll question your statements; so be very sure of your facts.

5. Prepare for the meeting by anticipating as many questions as you can, and have your answers ready.

6. Remember you can call on your SEA to address your colleagues. They're prophets from another country and thus more honored than you who labor in the local vineyard.

7. Make an appointment with individual administrators to discuss specific jobs incumbent on them; e.g., the superintendent's presentation to the school board of the application for PL 94-142 funds, or the part a district administrator might play in the handicapped child census.

A Blueprint for Getting Individual Schools Involved

One of your major jobs is implementing PL 94-142 in your district schools. Prepare to meet some resistance because you'll be invading school territory with that fearful weapon called "More Work" — and for people already carrying a full load. The building administration and staff want to help children, including the handicapped, but they would just as soon look the other way when they see you come in wearing that big 94-142 smile. Yet, the law has to be enacted, so you tackle the job.

A list of responsibilities, such as the one presented below, will help. You can adjust it to your particular needs, use it as a springboard for your work with building personnel — or you can develop your own list of building responsibilities. Once you have clearly in mind what the building jobs are, you will be better able to see how the work can get done. Furthermore, you may be able to spot situations where you are doing too little or too much; where you're taking on work that rightly belongs to the building staff, or vice versa.

APPLYING PL 94-142 IN THE DISTRICT SCHOOLS

BUILDING-STAFF JOBS	ASSISTANCE OF SPECIAL EDUCATION ADMINISTRATOR
1. Inform personnel of 94-142 requirements.	Meet with staff as needed to explain the law, especially the IEP.
2. Screen for special education services.	Provide screening format. Be on call as resource person.
3. Evaluate child using mental ability, achievement and diagnostic tests — in child's native language if best. Also, medical diagnosis.	Secure bilingual services where necessary. Help provide and monitor tests.
4. Get written parental consent for evaluation and placement of the child.	Convene parents' meeting to explain their part in child's special education.
5. Organize IEP teams. Grant released time for meetings.	Help set up schedules, and assist at meetings as needed.
6. Involve parents in their child's IEP. Keep records of efforts.	Handle special cases. Liaison between school and parents.
7. Implement least restrictive environment. Provide an array of services and settings.	Provide inservice on LRE. Liaison between regular and special education.
8. Set up schedules for support staff; e.g., itinerant teachers, physical therapists, and speech pathologists.	Provide input when schedules are being decided. Liaison work as needed.

9. Provide school health and social-work service for handicapped.	Input to school nurse and social workers about services needed for handicapped.
10. Provide special transportation.	Join school personnel in planning transportation. Handle difficult cases.
11. Gather information for district reports to SEA; e.g., child census and personnel needs.	Provide information on jobs to be done. Route forms to SEA.
12. Where appropriate, participate in a consolidated application for funding under PL 94-142.	Explain benefits of a consortium. Liaison between district and SEA.
13. Incorporate the confidentiality requirements under PL 94-142.	Explain these requirements to building staff. Help monitor implementation.
14. Employ other procedural safeguards; e.g., due process hearings, surrogate parents, and record keeping.	Explain safeguards, as needed. Help with specific cases.
15. Provide for professional growth.	Help with inservice programs, planning and delivery.

The above jobs aren't necessarily done by staff in each separate building. They can be shared. For example, a speech teacher will be the IEP person in speech for all the buildings she serves. The same will be the case for the psychological examiner, the school nurse, and so on. The point we're making is that in each building there are certain jobs that must be done, and it's up to the building administrator, working with the administrator of special education, to see that the requirements are met.

Breaking the Restricted Environment Barrier

A few months into the school year a regular fourth grade teacher exclaims, "I've got these kids, now what do I do with them? Our superintendent says, 'You have to take them; it's the law.' But I've never worked with kids this handicapped before!"

The teacher aired the problem in a rather abrupt fashion, but there's a lot to be said for the concern she voiced. In cases such as the one above, a superintendent has gone ahead and instructed all schools in his district to admit all students who live within the school boundaries, no matter what the handicapping condition of the students might be. At times this has been done out of fear of reprisal regarding the least restrictive environment mandated under PL 94-142. Unfortunately, administrators who do this don't understand the meaning of least restrictive environment (LRE).

The fact is that total integration into the regular school program isn't for all children. PL 94-142 indicates clearly that the least restrictive environment means a handicapped child is to be educated with children who are not handicapped, to the extent that the handicapped child benefits from this integration. When the child cannot benefit from regular classes the district is required to place him in an appropriate environment where he can benefit. Regular class placement is the ideal, but not always the reality.

Appropriate educational environment will vary for different children, so a district must consider an array of educational channels. The chart in Figure 8-1 illustrates various channels (settings) through which an education program can be delivered.

In Figure 8-1 the two-way flow of arrows indicates that no child needs to be, nor should be, locked into any one of the educational settings. Each of the boxes has arrows leading out from it to other settings. The most restrictive setting, the full-time special class without any integration (shown in top row, fourth box from the left), is becoming a rarity. Besides showing alternative settings, the figure presents some support services, such as speech and physical therapy. When projected on an overhead, the chart is helpful in explaining to regular educators what is involved in delivering special education in an appropriate environment.

In the beginning of this section we talked about a superintendent who integrated everyone. The reverse situation is just as inappropriate. Despite the law and the efforts of special educators, there are children in segrated situations who could profit from placement in regular classrooms. Perhaps the greatest barrier to this placement was voiced by the teacher quoted above — the lack of preparation to teach the handicapped on the part of regular teachers. Through no fault of their own, the majority of teachers in regular classes simply

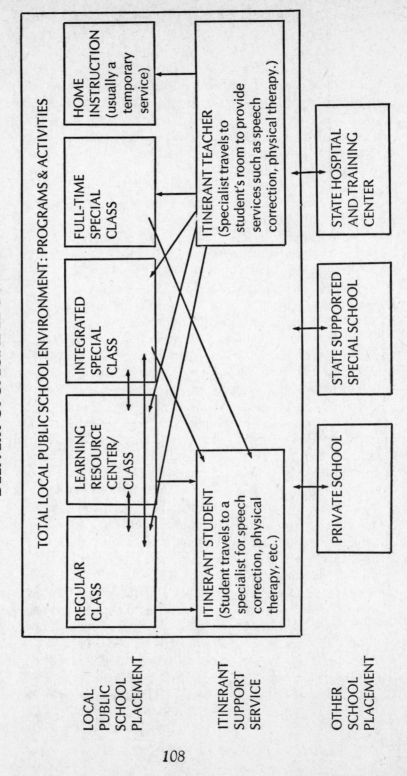

Figure 8-1
**AN ARRAY OF SETTINGS FOR
DELIVERY OF SPECIAL EDUCATION**

TOTAL LOCAL PUBLIC SCHOOL ENVIRONMENT: PROGRAMS & ACTIVITIES

HOME
INSTRUCTION
(usually a
temporary
service)

FULL-TIME
SPECIAL
CLASS

INTEGRATED
SPECIAL
CLASS

LEARNING
RESOURCE
CENTER/
CLASS

REGULAR
CLASS

ITINERANT TEACHER
(Specialist travels to
student's room to provide
services such as speech
correction, physical therapy.)

ITINERANT STUDENT
(Student travels to a
specialist for speech
correction, physical
therapy, etc.)

STATE HOSPITAL
AND TRAINING
CENTER

STATE SUPPORTED
SPECIAL SCHOOL

PRIVATE SCHOOL

LOCAL
PUBLIC
SCHOOL
PLACEMENT

ITINERANT
SUPPORT
SERVICE

OTHER
SCHOOL
PLACEMENT

do not have the understanding and techniques, at this time, to take on the responsibility of teaching handicapped children. Appropriate inservice and preservice courses are ways to help regular educators out of this difficulty.

The Art of Special Education Training for Regular Educators

You can come at this job from a number of directions. The art of handling special education inservice courses for regular educators is in the developmental stage; and thus far no one is sure of the way to go. The timing of your entry into the regular education area probably rests with the level of preparedness the regular educators have reached to accept direction from special education. We'll present some ways to provide the inservice, and some suggestions to interest regular teachers so they will want to take the courses offered. However, it will be up to you to pinpoint the opportune time for the initiation of the services. Here, then, are suggestions to prepare regular personnel for participation in special education courses:

1. Start with school administrators. Explain to them what the inservice will accomplish and why it should be done. Be brief, pleasant, to the point, and accurate. They should be informed of these regulations for inservice under PL 94-142:

    a. Inservice programs pertaining to PL 94-142 shall include regular teachers.

    b. Incentives which insure participation (salary-step credit, college credit, released time) are to be included in the inservice program.

    c. The inservice program shall include the identification of areas in which training is needed and a description of course content for each area.

2. Secure time to address the regular teachers about inservice, perhaps during a staff meeting. Tell them what you have previously told the administrators. Answer their questions or refer the questions to your SEA for clarification.

3. Later, talk informally with teachers about what they'd like for an inservice course. Write down this information, summarize it, and present it to the teachers as a group. Let them decide the particular area of inservice.

4. Keep in mind that local and state representatives of the National Education Association, and possibly representatives of the American Federation of Teachers, are also interested in the implications of PL 94-142 for regular educators. It might be well to ask these groups to a meeting where you'll be explaining PL 94-142 as it involves regular educators.

5. Formally tell the teachers about the specific inservice course you and a committee (possibly including your SEA) have worked out. In your communication, mention the incentives for participation your district allows.

6. If your SEA is using federal funds for personnel development courses, some of this money can be used for incentive purposes. You can discuss this with the SEA representative when the time arrives.

How to Act Within the Parameters of Your Authority

The best guide for understanding your parameters is a good job description — in writing. If a description doesn't exist, take time to make a rough draft of your job requirements as you perceive them: then submit it to your superior for his approval and editing. When this is done, write up a final draft and give a copy to your superior for his files. Refer to your job description when you question the appropriateness of some activity you're about to undertake.

On the other hand, it's not necessary — or even advantageous — to make a point of examining everything you do in the light of your written description, as you'll be called on to do many things not included in it. The criterion in cases like these is whether or not your activity will encroach on the actions and responsibilities of other staff members. Subtle perception checks regarding the impression you're making on colleagues will help you decide on what action to take — that, plus your own prudent judgment on when it's best to go ahead with something, no matter what feedback you're getting from your immediate audience.

In the face of all the responsiblities you now have, as compared to pre-PL 94-142 days, you may want to talk to your co-workers about the newness and multiplicity of your activities. Don't make a big thing of it. In fact, we suggest you weave this idea into another talk you might be giving. But speak frankly, telling your audience that you have no desire to encroach on the rights and duties of others as you carry out what has to be done under the new federal law. Should questions arise later as to who does what, ask your co-workers to talk with you about any overstepping of your boundaries, apparent or real.

If you can get this point across in a frank and sincere manner, you will have predisposed the people with whom you work to accept the widening area of responsibility of the administrator of special education.

The Importance of Imparting Exact Information

Time was when a district's policy was almost entirely of its own making. A misstatement by an administrator could be interpreted as "being something to do with that district's policy." With the onset of federal laws and regulations that spell out so minutely what shall and shall not be done in special education, the casual, individual method of implementing district programs is no longer permissible.

A distinct characteristic of the post-PL 94-142 special education administrator is his grasp of federal rules and regulations pertaining to this area; and his painstaking care in imparting and implementing this knowledge when and where it is needed. This acquisition is of prime importance because teachers, parents, advocates, and in some cases handicapped students themselves, are becoming increasingly aware that a statement made by the special education administrator can't be an "off-the-top-of-my-head" kind of communication. People feel free to question the authority and background of what you say regarding special education and related services in your district. Mistakes aren't glossed over. Credibility can easily be lost if you're not knowledgeable and careful when you give information and answer questions.

Another point to be made here is that the word "exact" doesn't just mean being correct, as opposed to incorrect, although that's its prime connotation. "Exact" also means precise and to the point, as opposed to a rambling sort of answer which tends to put people off, especially when the one questioned isn't sure of his response, or doesn't want to reply fully.

Summary

An important job for the administrator of special education is applying PL 94-142 to the regular school program. He must impart clear and accurate information to district administrators. Regular teachers depend on him to provide leadership and inservice on working with the handicapped. When doing these tasks, he must also be keenly aware of the parameters of his authority.

Chapter Nine

How Changes Required by PL 94-142 Are Applied to the Classroom

Before PL 94-142: "That's what it was to be alive. To move about in a cloud of ignorance...to spend and waste time as though you had a million years" (OUR TOWN, by Thornton Wilder).

If we never had PL 94-142, there would still have been changes in education, but we may not have had so many so soon. It's the rapidity and multiplicity of changes that are compounding the responsibilities of the administrator of special education, and the work of the classroom teacher. Previous to PL 94-142 the regular classroom was, for all intents and purposes, a self-contained unit of normal children being taught at a grade level (or subject-content level in the secondary school) which, comparatively speaking, allowed little flexibility.

PL 94-142 has changed this substantially. Let us examine those parts of the new law that pertain to the classroom:

IDENTIFYING CLASSROOM CHANGES

1. Today's regular classroom has students who are there because of the Education for All Handicapped Children Act (PL 94-142), which requires regular classroom placement for all children who can benefit there.

2. The added responsibility of handling specially designed instruction for the handicapped means a reduction in the number of students in some classrooms.

3. The teacher who has handicapped children in her classroom can request aids and materials needed to help these students obtain an appropriate education.

4. The regular teacher may need inservice programs to aid her in instructing the handicapped.

5. Special education personnel working out of the district office will meet, upon request, with the regular teacher to offer advice and to give direct assistance. These persons include the special education administrator, speech pathologist, physical therapist, and teachers of the deaf and blind.

6. Special education personnel, in a building where handicapped students are in regular classrooms, can be called on to:

   a. Inform the classroom teacher about appropriate learning materials for handicapped students.
   b. Help monitor students' progress.
   c. Join with the classroom teacher in reporting to parents.
   d. Observe handicapped children in the classroom and evaluate their progress and needs.

7. The classroom teacher can utilize the services of a resource room for those handicapped children who aren't benefitting from regular instruction.

8. The classroom teacher can refer to special education any student she suspects of being handicapped — and know that the child will be evaluated and given special services as needed.

9. The classroom teacher has a copy of each handicapped student's individualized education program, around which she builds instructional programs. In some cases she will have helped in the development of the IEP.

10. A sampling of students in today's schoolrooms resembles a cross section of our society more closely than a typical classroom did a few years ago, when children of different abilities were segregated from the mainstream for purposes of instruction.

11. A good result of these changes is that the classroom teacher and special education personnel are now working together. Instead of hearing "He's your student," from the regular teacher when referring to a handicapped child, the special education teacher can expect to hear, "He's ours." Or even, "He's mine."

12. These words will probably be spoken by regular teachers when the evolving concept of the place of the special educator finally takes hold — the provider of specially designed instruction. The regular classroom will be a self-fulfilling one for all children who can benefit there when the regular teacher sees herself as having ownership of all children.

There is one more point to be made here. It concerns the referral process mentioned in item 8 above. When planning inservice for regular teachers, include a course on the characteristics of children who should be referred for special education. Teachers have a tendency to refer children who are either disruptive or so obviously handicapped that there is no doubt as to their eligibility. Other children who may be handicapped are overlooked because they are thought to be lazy, or disinterested, or quiet, obedient plodders who just naturally have a hard time in school.

Teachers should be asking these questions: Is the lazy child hard of hearing or visually impaired? Is the quiet non-achiever in need of counseling? Can the inattentive child be helped in a learning disabled program? When teachers are informed about what to look for, they will be more comfortable in making referrals, and their input regarding the child's learning problems will be improved.

Classroom Changes Start
with School Principals

In the monograph, *Instructional Alternatives for Exceptional Children* (Deno, 1973), Maynard Reynolds, Professor in the Department of Special Education at the University of Minnesota, has this to say regarding the context for change in the area of special education:

> The assumption is incorrect that the delivery of special education services can be transformed directly and easily from, for example, a special-class model to a resource room or consulting

teacher model, simply by training and inserting new personnel in unchanged schools and systems. To make the transformation, fundamental changes are required, changes that involve educational personnel, parents, universities and state departments of education. Some of the ways in which such persons and institutions are involved are as follows:

> Changes in special education must be understood and supported by school principals and other administrators....

Dr. Reynolds goes on to list a number of other persons who are important in changing special education. However, the first person mentioned on his list is the school principal.

Another confirmation of the principal's importance as a factor in change was emphasized during a recent meeting of educators at an institute on mainstreaming. Of the top twelve issues discussed, the highest consideration was given to the one which stated, "Mainstreaming of the handicapped must have the understanding and active cooperation of the building principal if it is to succeed."

Yet another example of the crucial position held by this administrator, this time given in more general terms, is in this quotation by William L. Smith, Associate Commissioner, National Center for the Improvement of Educational Systems. In his preface to *Instructional Alternatives for Exceptional Children* (Deno, 1973) Dr. Smith makes this statement:

> New training designs should not serve teachers alone, however. Only if they embrace administrators and the full range of professional personnel in the schools can they guarantee the establishment of a climate that is marked by basic humanism which provides each child with an identifiable, individualized path to learning experiences.

The point we're making here is that the groundwork for necessary changes in school buildings is laid during your meetings with building principals. In districts where integration of the handicapped hasn't been promulgated by the principal, teachers have to cope with extra work, as the following example points out:

> In a certain school, each time the special education teacher sees that a student is ready to be integrated, she finds it necessary to approach the appropriate regular teachers, one by one, to see who will take the child. She has to explain the law and answer all questions regarding the problems of placing the handicapped in a regular class. Regular educators have received no informa-

tion nor directives from their principal, so feel little job responsibility for undertaking the task, although many understand the predicament the special educator is in and take on the extra pupil. But they do it because, "Mary (the special education teacher) is such a good person," or "Gee, she'd do the same for me," or "It sounds as if this student can really make it. I'll go ahead and give him a chance. Mary is too good a teacher to recommend a student unless she were sure," or "Mary says it's the law if it's on his IEP."

This isn't as it should be. The reasons shouldn't be personal, nor should they be the result of one person's opinion, or good-heartedness. Teachers respond to directives from their principal. They feel comfortable only when he informs them of procedures whereby special education personnel can confer with them about placement of handicapped children in regular classrooms.

How to Motivate Teachers
Toward Change

Let's assume the principal has given his support to implementing the least restrictive environment mandate. Now it's your responsibility to motivate the teachers toward putting the mandate into efficient action. To begin with, every teacher needs to know what is expected of her in this operation. Studies have shown that when the expectations of administrators aren't met, the usual reason is that teachers don't know what is expected of them before they are asked to go ahead with a task. Knowledge is the first requirement. But concomitant with giving information, you also want to motivate. Do this step-by-step. In special education the miracles come after long, hard work. Here is a case in point:

In a school where both the district and building administrators had given much support to the development of a resource room, the special education personnel were finding much passive resistance to the new concept by regular teachers. They had accepted the handicapped into their rooms because their superior had told them they must. But where they had a chance to demonstrate resistance they did so by refusing to patronize the resource room. This went on for a good three weeks before the special education people realized what was happening. Then they got busy:

1. They (including the special education administrator) personally talked with each classroom teacher who seemed the least bit interested in seeing what the resource room could do for students who needed special instruction.
2. They had already established a good program, but they made it even better. It was redone so that every interested person could see what was going on when he visited the room. Packets for the attainment of numerous instructional goals were arranged on a rack similar to a magazine display. Charts, ready for children's names, dates of entry, goals to be achieved, measurement data, and dates of exit, were displayed.
3. The final hurdle was cleared when the regular teachers were invited to send their most difficult students to the resource room. Some teachers broke the resistance barrier at this point and truly sent their greatest problems; children who needed behavior modification as well as special academic instruction. The resource people did such a fine job that from then on the program was slated for success. At future IEP meetings the regular staff sincerely considered the resource room as an alternative setting.

There are a number of observations to be drawn from this account:

1. The resource room people had the full support of the special education administrator. Left on their own they may have hesitated to take the initiative in doing as much as they did. It shows what you and your staff can accomplish when working together.
2. At times the direction given by the principal isn't enough to put across a new idea. In the above example an important ingredient for success was initially missing: the teachers' support.
3. It took extraordinary means to change the teachers' attitude. Although we have said that it shouldn't be necessary to approach teachers individually, there are times when your strategy is to do what will work, regardless of previous decisions.

4. An administrator of special education has to be able to say to himself, "I know this is a good innovation, and I'm going to see that it works."

5. Finally, people — teachers included — will not respond wholeheartedly to a change brought about solely by outside directives. Some inner direction for action is required.

Tips on Providing Classroom Help During a Time of Change

For the special education staff:

1. Review with your teachers, as needed, the changes brought about under PL 94-142. For example, as the time approaches for first-time participation in an IEP meeting, see that the teacher knows the procedures your district has drawn up for the development of a child's IEP.

2. Recall that progress is made by small steps forward, noted and given recognition. The teacher's goal is total implementation of PL 94-142; but don't let that picture shroud the small achievements that lead toward it.

3. Don't expect all teachers to move forward at the same rate. Because some go slower than others, this doesn't necessarily mean they all won't reach the goal.

4. When special education teachers change from the self-contained model to a resource room:

   a. Check their credentials. To go from teaching in one category, e.g., the mentally retarded, to teaching children with a variety of handicaps, requires a credential change.

   b. Help them plan the program and equip the room. (See "Hints for Helping the Resource Room Teacher," in Chapter 7.)

   c. See that each person's responsibilities and time schedule are worked out. All involved should know exactly what is expected.

   d. Provide teachers the opportunity to visit resource rooms in other buildings or districts, and to attend workshops concerned with this model.

e. Encourage resource room teachers to apply for federal grants. Innovative grants are often awarded to programs that operate on the resource room model. It lends itself to creativity.

Regular teachers who are instructing handicapped children also need your assistance in time of change:

1. Offer your advice and direct help. But be wary of coming forward too quickly. Being over-eager to correct can be disconcerting to experienced educators and overwhelming to the neophyte.

2. Keep in mind that problems will be solved as regular teachers profit from inservice, workshops, and conferences. This excerpt from a conference, titled *The Classroom Teacher and PL 94-142*, points out how shared experiences can help:

Some participants were teachers already working with the handicapped. They said they were apprehensive at first that they would be called on to do more than they could handle. That they'd be scrutinized too closely, and rated too harshly. They agreed these concerns disappeared with the realization of how effective the IEP approach is. One teacher put it this way. "No one can say an individual teacher is too hard, or too easy, when developing a child's education program. It's a team decision, made by people involved in the child's whole life. I think it's wonderful."

A gratifying way to help teachers accommodate the demands of PL 94-142 is to go over the following list with them. The items are clear to you, but perhaps obscure to others. Try them out on a few regular teachers and you'll see what we mean. You can add to the list, but for a start see that your district's teachers can react positively to this information:

1. Their school district provides special education to handicapped children in the following age range; ____ to ____ years. (The range will vary according to state statutes, etc.)

2. Written parental consent is obtained whenever the district undertakes (a) evaluation of a child who is, or is suspected of being, handicapped; and (b) the initial placement of a child in special education.

3. Written notice is given to parents before the district changes, or refuses to change, the identification or educational placement of a handicapped child.

4. Parents are invited to their child's IEP meeting, and encouraged to participate.

5. Parents have the right to examine all records pertaining to their handicapped child, and to request amendments and changes in the records as they see fit.

The above list is a start toward helping the classroom teacher get a grasp on what is involved in the PL 94-142 law in her district.

You won't be supervising regular class teachers. But should they request assistance, there are certain procedures to follow:

A request for you to observe a student should be followed by a conference on your observations, just as for your special education staff. It isn't enough to stand at the back of the classroom and talk with the teacher; in fact, any conversation during class time should be discouraged. The teacher will respect your professional opinion much more if she knows you will observe the child, reflect on what you have observed, and then meet with her to discuss the situation.

On occasion, teachers may ask about certain students when they see you in the school hall. This is perfectly all right. But here again, we suggest you follow up with a more formal response, such as described above.

A final word: The parameters of your authority in the area of regular education are not yet clearly defined. And until the time comes when they are, the special administrator moves carefully into this field, and only when his aid is requested.

How to React to Roadblocks

Decisions influencing the organization and delivery of special education are made at the top, by legislation. The actual carrying out of the IEP program is done by the teachers. You're the man in the middle, and there are times when you run into roadblocks no matter where you turn. Let's take some of the mandates in PL 94-142 and see what you can do if their implementation seems blocked.

1. A section on the Individualized Education Program deals with parent participation. A number of your IEPs lack parent involvement, although the district's efforts toward this end are well documented. What can you do?

   One solution is to let the matter stand. The rules and regulations are being followed. The results aren't successful, but that doesn't imply negligence.

   Another reaction would be to undertake solution activities on your own. What follows are suggestions along this line:

   a. Confer with a parent on the phone. Place the call or write a note asking the parent to phone your office at his convenience.

   b. Make a home visit. You will decide if it's better to make an appointment or just drop in.

   c. When you've made contact, explain what the IEP meeting entails and the parent's right to help plan his child's educational program. The information you give will cause a significant number of parents to participate in further IEP meetings.

2. A frequent roadblock is met when special education administrators ask for more help for their teachers. Assume you've asked for a resource room aide and your request wasn't granted. What can you do?

   a. You can let the status quo remain and keep on asking for more help, thinking that if you alleviate the situation with volunteer services, which are of poor quality at this time, your superior may never agree that more paid help is needed.

   b. You can talk the situation over with the teacher to see what can be done by way of upgrading volunteer services.

   c. You can flatly state to your superior that the work load in the resource room is unrealistic and it is your suggestion that numbers be reduced until more help is available.

In summary, when roadblocks are met:

1. Think what will happen two or three steps ahead before taking the first step.

2. Accept the fact you won't be able to remove all barriers, despite your efforts.

3. Take on those that are the most important, not too many at a time, and work out solutions that have the approval of your superiors. The chain-of-command has to be followed as long as you work in an organization.

4. After due thought, if you decide to do nothing about a situation, remember that this is a decision too — perhaps the best one at the time you make it.

When to Employ a Holding Pattern

There will be times when you'll be ready to finalize some activity, but for reasons beyond your control you have to hold off. It's similar to the pilot's situation after he's made the Atlantic trip in perfect flying time and comes in for a landing only to be told that local conditions necessitate his being placed in a 5-hour holding pattern.

Implementing special education can be just as disconcerting, as these cases exemplify:

1. It's been decided that a classroom in your district will be assigned to the program for the seriously emotionally disturbed. It's a bright, sunny room and you are looking forward to hiring a good teacher you've had in mind. Unfortunately, a spring pre-registration shows such an increase in enrollment that the principal says he'll need that room for an added fifth-grade section. He says your program can locate in a former faculty room. It's small, and the windows are high so one can't look out. Cupboard and counter space is lacking.

   You have a number of things to consider here:
   a. Hold off making any move until every possibility has been explored that might lead to a better facility.
   b. If school starts and you're still not satisfied with the facility, continue to hold off starting the program.
   c. To remain adamant until professional requirements are met will result in your demands for excellence being handled in a more serious manner than would

occur if you simply voiced your opinion and then took what was offered.

2. Here's another case. The school board has asked you what the district should do in regard to providing and instructing surrogate parents. You research all available material, but you're not clear on the requirements. Your state educational agency informs you that they can't advise, as they, too, are working on the problem. The Bureau of Education for the Handicapped in Washington D.C. hasn't any specific guidelines. What to do? Here's one answer:

Reject the idea of giving an incomplete report; and put yourself into a holding pattern until you have sufficient information to present to your board. On the day you were to give the report, explain your position. It's important to keep in mind that a holding pattern doesn't necessarily mean you're not acting on the problem. On the contrary you can work on it a great deal; gathering information, conferring with your superiors and others involved, and figuring out when the most opportune time to act will be.

3. Another case involves a parent who won't sign a consent agreement to have his child evaluated. The district may use the due process procedure to force consent, but every administrator knows this would be a last resort — and possibly a lost cause as far as providing a comfortable atmosphere for the child's education, since hearings often result in hard feelings. So you hold off using legal means. Meanwhile, you make every effort to help the parent see how evaluation, and possibly specially designed instruction, will help his child.

To summarize, let us go back to the pilot who holds his plane in mid-air while waiting for the correct time to land. Your holding pattern is also one that waits for the correct time for certain actions. And you use that time well. This makes you more precise, more sure of what you are doing, and more valuable, in the long run, to your district.

Summary

Both regular and special teachers need assistance from the special education administrator during a time of change. Meanwhile, the support of building principals is a factor which can't be overlooked. The administrator of special education must lay plans to circumvent roadblocks. In some cases he should be able to maintain a holding pattern on implementing special education until professional requirements are met.

Chapter Ten

The Special Education Administrator and Classroom Teaching

To whom an administrator is readily available and in what areas an administrator spends his time telegraph distinct non-verbal messages to the staff.

Your leadership as an administrator of special education emerges in a multiplicity of situations. However, in no other area is your expertise as important as it is in the instructional field, where one of your prime responsibilities is to become increasingly knowledgeable about what constitutes good classroom teaching.

The material which follows pertains to characteristics that teachers of all children should possess. The boundaries of the special branch of education have been redrawn and enlarged. They now include the regular education system to the extent that many regular classroom teachers are implementing the "specially designed instruction" developed for the handicapped. What we used to expect from good special education teachers, we now must expect from all.

Characteristics of Good Teachers for All Children

The abilities demonstrated by a competent classroom teacher come from within herself. Her personal behavior pattern shows that she is working at becoming or maintaining herself as a person who:

1. Is aware of her own strengths and weaknesses.
2. Has confidence in her ability to succeed.
3. Fosters a capacity for change within herself in terms of openness to new concepts and experiences.
4. Recognizes the limits of her competencies in order to make referral decisions.
5. Has the capacity to work independently when an appropriate level of competence has been achieved.
6. Accepts each child with respect to the educational and emotional needs he demonstrates.

The administrator of special education will also observe that a competent teacher has the ability to:

1. Record with accuracy children's behavior in various settings.
2. Distinguish between normal and deviant behavior within a child and between children.
3. Identify problems in the affective area; for example, problems in adjustment to school routines, or the inability to relate with peers.
4. Identify problems in the psychomotor area; for example, problems in integrating eye-hand movements.
5. Establish a rich learning environment for an individual or group of learners.
6. Assist individuals to gain behavioral control; for example, to increase attention span, be less distracting, control inappropriate speech.

In the instructional area, the competent teacher demonstrates the ability to:

1. Write behavioral objectives that specify what a child will be able to do at the end of an instruction period.
2. Assess and describe in behavioral terms the level of academic performance, the social adjustment, and the motor performance of children she has been teaching.
3. Pinpoint areas of strengths and weaknesses in a child's reading, math, and language skills.
4. Use data from test results in planning instruction.
5. Design informal activities for individual assessment.

6. Develop lesson plans that lead toward the attainment of the short and long term goals developed by the IEP team.

7. Provide appropriate curriculum for particular age groups; for example, low vocabulary/high interest reading material for the older mentally retarded student.

8. Prepare teacher-made materials, when necessary, for the instruction of a particular individual or group.

9. Efficiently utilize commercially prepared materials.

10. Break down a lesson (reading, math, health) into discrete sequential steps in order to analyze, and correct if necessary, a student's learning behavior as he proceeds with the learning task.

11. Continuously diagnose the performance of the student during instruction and make adjustments to meet his needs.

12. Teach to the educational needs of the child, rather than, for example, a trainable mentally retarded program — or any other categorical program.

13. Utilize the principles of reinforcement in order to increase desired behavior or eliminate undesirable behavior.

In the area of professional functioning, the competent teacher shows her ability to:

1. Work with other staff members in a supportive manner, accept and value differences, and seek the development of positive working relationships among her colleagues.

2. Provide, in the area of her expertise, consulting and support services to other teachers in regular or special classrooms, whatever the case might be.

3. Establish rapport with parents to the extent that she and the parents can share information which helps promote a child's academic, social, and emotional growth.

4. Adapt to changes in the profession; for example, the changes brought about by PL 94-142 — and for regular teachers, the fact that some supervision of their teaching will be done by special education personnel.

Most, if not all, of these fine characteristics are within the grasp of all teachers. Many already demonstrate the qualities. Others can demonstrate them but don't. Teachers in this group need leadership from an administrator. They will respond to a person who frankly, but diplomatically, lets them know they have more of the qualities of an excellent educator than they are demonstrating.

A third group of teachers lacks a significant number of the above characteristics. A personnel development program for these educators should be planned around the areas of greatest need in the listings. However, in the case of regular educators the special education supervisor can't do much more than observe these shortcomings. Yet, the inevitability that the special education supervisor will be working with regular teachers in their classrooms makes it important for him to begin to perceive what the needs for the handicapped are in the regular program.

Special Classroom Requirements for the Handicapped

The special education administrator can share the following information with teachers on an individual basis, or present it to a group. He can also use it as a checklist when observing in rooms where handicapped students are enrolled — especially in regular classrooms. We'll itemize the requirements according to the handicapped condition:

1. Deaf, Deaf-blind, Hard of Hearing:
    a. Itinerant teacher of the deaf
    b. Placement in the room where they can lip read
    c. Sufficient light for lip reading
    d. Hearing aids
    e. Careful instruction in emergency procedures
    f. Subtitles on classroom sound-films
    g. Special instruction regarding their impairment
    h. Knowledge of resources relevant to their impairment

2. Mentally Retarded:
    a. Specially designed instruction
    b. Low teacher/pupil ratio
    c. Classroom aide where teacher/pupil ratio is high
    d. Special equipment and materials related to instruction
    e. Special assistance with appearance and personal hygiene
    f. Careful instruction in emergency procedures

3. Multihandicapped, Orthopedically and Other Health Impaired:

    a. Specially designed desks, chairs, standing boards, ramps, lavatories, sinks, drinking fountains, latches, scissors and other manipulative instruments

    b. Removal of architectural barriers

    c. Information regarding their impairment, where appropriate

    d. Knowledge of resources relevant to their impairment

    e. Teacher informed about medications

4. Seriously Emotionally Disturbed:

    a. Teacher psychologically prepared to work with this group

    b. Removal from pressure situations

    c. An aide to help manage behavior improvement

    d. Part time school attendance in some cases

5. Specific Learning Disability:

    a. Specially designed instruction

    b. Removal of distractions

    c. Low teacher/pupil ratio

6. Speech Impaired:

    a. Speech pathologist's program carried on in the classroom

    b. Reinforcement procedures wherever appropriate

7. Visually Impaired:

    a. Placement which insures best visual advantage

    b. Large print books

    c. Itinerant teacher of the visually impaired

    d. Careful instruction in emergency procedures

    e. Special instruction regarding their impairment

    f. Knowledge of resources relevant to their impairment

Regular classroom teachers, as well as special teachers, should be aware of the above information. We include special teachers because many of them, having had experience in only one area of special education; for example, the teachers of the mentally retarded, now find themselves assigned to a resource room where they instruct children with many kinds of handicaps.

Six Ways You Can Help
Improve Classroom Instruction

There is no doubt that improvement of instruction is the most rewarding activity you can undertake. Here are some ways to accomplish this:

1. Lead a group of teachers in a discussion about setting realistic instructional goals for the handicapped. Include goals set for children at various academic levels, and with varying handicapping conditions. For example:

    Take the evaluation information and diagnostic data on a pupil, block out the personally identifiable material, and work with your teachers to establish instructional goals. Where necessary, present all the characteristics of the student's handicapping condition which might affect his learning.

2. Help teachers adapt present curriculum to fit handicapped students. For example:

    Mathematics which involve story problems written at too young a level for the older mentally retarded student can be restated to fit the higher interest level.

3. Help in the search for interesting teaching material that is on a horizontal level. For example:

    A child may take months to learn to tell time. Varied instructional materials are needed at each step in order to keep him interested.

4. Aid in the development of educational media centers. For example:

    Working with your resource room teacher, evaluate existing centers in terms of what is useful for the handicapped. Then compile a list of additional media needed by your program and work with regular media center personnel in fulfilling these needs.

5. Inform teachers of available support services and secure the services where necessary. For example:

    A high school teacher realizes she should give more attention to her work-experience program but hasn't time to investigate community resources. You can do three things:

(a) share what information you have about the community, (b) put her in touch with the local Vocation Rehabilitation Division office, or (c) discuss the program with the school's regular work-experience coordinator to see what help is available there.

6. Assist in scheduling students into support service programs. For example:

A classroom teacher appreciates knowing: (a) how many openings there are in a support service, (b) approximately when she can expect service for her students, (c) that her students' classroom program is considered when scheduling is done, (d) that no schedule is inflexible, and (e) that the administrator of special education checks periodically to see that arrangements are satisfactory.

How to Help with Children Who Have Behavior Problems

To coin a phrase, "Help the child; for when his behavior problem is taken care of the teacher will no longer need help." Of course this can't be taken literally, because in nine cases out of ten you'll help the child by going through the teacher. The point is, though, that if your help starts and ends with the teacher it might be ineffective. So when you are asked to help with a behavior problem, our first suggestion is to observe the child and satisfy yourself that his trouble doesn't stem from a handicapping condition which needs special education. After this, there are a number of approaches to alleviate poor behavior.

Early intervention helps ward off crises, as this innovative program demonstrates:

In a district where a cluster of schools has persistent problems, a strong, sympathetic person, preferably with training in counseling, is appointed to work with students in both regular and special education. When a behavior incident occurs she is called to focus in on the disruptive child. If he is unable to function in the classroom, she removes him temporarily, talks with him, counsels him, and confers with parents when necessary. At times she might take over the class that has been disrupted while the teacher takes the child aside to talk with him. The crisis person does not take sides in the disturbance; nor does she punish or sanction the child in any way. She maintains a low profile. Students don't view her as a person in charge of discipline. Ideally, they aren't able to categorize her at all. "The lady who comes when there's trouble with X," is probably the best way to describe her.

Sometimes classroom problems result from inadequacies on the part of the teacher. Here are some helpful hints:

1. During post-observation conferences with the teacher, go over the areas that need strengthening if better room management is to take place.

2. Provide consultation, intervention services, or inservice courses that focus on room management.

3. Give the list of fine characteristics at the beginning of this chapter to the teacher for self-evaluation. She'll diagnose her weaknesses and take steps to strengthen them, asking for help when she needs it.

4. Make an original list of things you observe in the classroom that appear to lessen control. Discuss them with the teacher. Following are some examples:

   The teacher: a. Talks too much.

   b. Doesn't utilize voice control; talks too loudly or too softly.

   c. Doesn't follow through with procedures for student conduct.

   d. Hasn't involved students in development of procedures for student conduct.

   e. Has no procedures for student conduct.

   f. Has too many procedures for student conduct. (The students are so involved in "rules of order" that the room often erupts in loud arguments and disagreements over minor infringements.)

5. Work with the teacher in drafting short term objectives for students who are learning correct behavior.

   "Sandy will be able to participate satisfactorily in our daily class meeting," is similar to, "Sandy will be able to sound the consonant 'm' when presented with the letter m." In each case the teacher states the goal, then works out the tasks for its attainment. In the case of the class meeting, Sandy can be kept on target by having responsibilities such as:

    a. Giving a short report pertaining to the meeting.
    b. Keeping a tally of individual student participation.
    c. Summarizing the meeting.

Six Ways for Teachers to Achieve and Maintain Outstanding Success

The successful teacher possesses a significant number of the characteristics discussed in the foregoing material. Yet, to be an outstanding success (we're accenting the word "outstanding"), she should work toward these additional attributes:

1. The ability to explain her program to the public. The outstanding teacher is so enthusiastic about her work that she has no hesitancy in discussing it with others who are interested in what she's doing. She can address parent groups, staff personnel, and community organizations.

2. The desire and ability to adopt promising educational practices and materials proven effective through research and demonstration. This educational practice is a regulation under PL 94-142. However, the outstanding teacher does it because she's interested in improving her program. She doesn't need a law to direct her.

3. Active participation in professional organizations. The superior educator contributes to educational societies of which she is a member. She may write articles for professional publications. And she reads educational material related to a number of teaching areas in addition to her own specific field.

4. The organizational ability to utilize the time and talents of paraprofessionals. The outstanding teacher has made a study of good management procedures. She trains her aides and utilizes their talents in a way that makes them enjoy working in her classroom.

5. The ability to challenge students to greater and greater accomplishment until they rise above what is expected of

them. Her teaching isn't lessened by putting a cap on the handicapped students' level of achievement.

6. The ability to "draw the line" when necessary. The superior teacher demonstrates that teaching is her prime interest and responsibility. Only when her classroom responsibilities are carried out in an excellent manner will she become involved in the "extras." Her students come first.

Administrative Factors That Influence Classroom Teaching

We've talked at length about your working with teachers for improved instruction. The following information lists things you can do on your own to improve the classroom operation.

1. See that instructional materials and equipment are easily accessible.
   a. Set up a charge account in a neighborhood store for necessities such as cooking and sewing supplies. Pattern it after the school's home economics purchasing procedures.
   b. Foresee, and forestall if necessary, problems special education might have in checking out materials and equipment. There are building administrators who believe all supplies and equipment for special education are provided by special education funds. (These funds provide only what is needed over and above regular school supplies.)
   c. Set up a yearly expense budget for each special teacher for items not available from the school or district storeroom.

2. Check into the classroom when a substitute teacher is present. Some handicapped children have difficulty in adapting to new teachers. They respond positively to the presence, even for a brief time, of someone they recognize. This is especially true of mentally retarded children.

3. Be present when a teacher is having open house. It shows the teacher, her building colleagues, and parents, that you are actively interested in this teacher's program.

4. Let your teachers know you are available to answer questions when they are explaining their program and room

management procedures to parents and other qualified persons.

5. Let your teachers know you'll assist them in setting up guidelines for:
   a. Visitors to their classrooms.
   b. Parent conferences.
   c. Unscheduled classroom interruptions.

These "assists" can make a difference in the way teachers feel about working in your district. When you take an interest in alleviating situations that bother teachers, but aren't serious enough to come to a crisis, you have gone the extra mile. And you'll find it's worth it.

Key Factors in Developing a Mainstreaming Package

After her child had been taken from a self-contained room for the mentally retarded and placed back in the regular classroom, a mother wrote this letter to the governor of her state:

> Dear Governor,
>
> I don't want any more mainstreaming for my child. She was doing well in her special class when five months ago they took her out of there and put her in the regular room. She's gone backwards ever since. She was learning her ABC's and how to cut with a scissors and was starting to learn how to read before they moved her. Now she just sits. Where have all the special teachers gone? We pay taxes for our schools, and we want one for our little girl.
>
>   Signed, Mrs. _____, a concerned parent.

Proper preparation, follow-through, and follow-up are necessary where handicapped students are assigned to regular classrooms. Unfortunately, this isn't always done — as the above letter illustrates.

Public Law 94-142 makes no mention of mainstreaming. The educational setting referred to is called least restrictive environment (LRE), which implies a number of educational settings. A child who is homebound is in quite a restricted environment, as is a child who is institutionalized, or hospitalized. Yet these environments — temporarily at least — are best suited to present needs.

Handicapped children placed in a non-restricted environment

(the mainstream), are those attending regular schools. But even here, the degree of mainstreaming should be determined for each child. For some, a mainstreaming program may be having lunch and recess with normal peers. Other handicapped children may spend the whole day in the regular program, receiving special services in regular classrooms. Children vary in the degree they benefit from mainstreaming. Here are some considerations:

1. Mainstream involvement should be decided during the student's IEP meeting.
2. A handicapped student, transferred to a regular classroom, needs to be individually prepared for the change.
3. Adaptation of curriculum and classroom procedures are often necessary to meet the handicapped student's needs.
4. Mainstreaming should not be initiated for large groups at a time.
5. Parents should know why their child is moved from the protected setting of the self-contained classroom.
6. Mainstreaming helps dispel the stigma often attached to the self-contained classroom.

A mainstreaming program that is carefully planned and carried out will see many benefits occur. Some guidelines for school personnel are necessary, however. They are presented in the material which follows:

GUIDELINES FOR ADMINISTRATORS

1. Be current on legislation and litigation that pertain to special education, particularly to a student's right to the least restrictive environment.
2. Provide impetus for mainstreaming, or be part of the group that instigates this.
3. If mainstreaming programs are already in operation, evaluate them and work with your staff to increase their efficacy.
4. Provide inservice programs on all aspects of mainstreaming pertinent to your district.
5. Retain a special education back-up program for students who cannot benefit from regular programs.

6. Be so oriented that school children are characterized by educational learning descriptors rather than by handicapping category.

7. Share the following jobs with building principals.

GUIDELINES FOR BUILDING PRINCIPALS

1. Participate with the administrator of special education in carrying out the above tasks.

2. Utilize resources for mainstreaming presently available within your staff.

3. Be available to answer questions asked by teachers and others involved in the mainstream program.

4. Arrange teachers' schedules so that those involved in mainstreaming will have time to communicate.

5. Be available as a liaison between the mainstreaming program and parents.

6. Establish good community relations relative to mainstreaming.

7. Appraise the performance of regular teachers who will be accepting handicapped students. A quality program of individualized instruction is essential.

8. Appraise the responsibilities of the special education teacher and the regular teacher using the following questions (which can be resolved during the IEP meeting):

   a. Who is responsible for the amount of time the students spend away from regular classrooms?

   b. Who updates the instructional program (goals, performance indicators, evaluation) of the students?

   c. Who reports to parents?

   d. Who keeps academic records? Who is keeping track of graduation requirements?

   e. How are students evaluated in regard to benefits (or non-benefits) of mainstreaming?

   f. What criteria are used to program students back into regular classes?

   g. In schools where all students are registered in regular classes, what criteria are used to send students to resource rooms?

GUIDELINES FOR TEACHERS OF SPECIAL CLASSROOMS WHO MAINSTREAM STUDENTS

1. Secure the support of the building principal before mainstreaming.
2. Be sure regular teachers have information about mainstreaming, before integrating students.
3. Keep a record of students' progress in the regular room.
4. Participate in keeping parents informed about their child's progress.
5. Obtain information regarding the students' behavior in the regular room. Suggested points for observation:
   a. Where are handicapped students sitting? Being placed in a way that sets them apart from class groupings may lead to social maladjustment.
   b. Are they able to respond to oral directions? Do they respond?
   c. Is the academic presentation sufficiently individualized?
   d. Is there observable, beneficial interaction among all students in the room?
6. Secure ongoing evaluation so that a decision can be made periodically as to whether to continue the integration.

GUIDELINES FOR RESOURCE ROOM TEACHERS

1. See that the areas you are going to help the child in are clearly specified. Goals should be developed at the IEP meeting.
2. See that pre- and post-tests are administered. If you are the one who administers the tests, share the results with regular teachers.
3. Be careful that the resource room doesn't become a one-way street. Return students to regular rooms as soon as a suitable learning situation can be offered.
4. Don't relinquish quality for quantity. No one benefits if too many students are assigned. Enough time and help should be provided so that each student can be instructed according to his needs.

GUIDELINES FOR REGULAR TEACHERS WHO TEACH HANDICAPPED CHILDREN

1. School districts that program handicapped children into the mainstream should insure that their regular teachers have:

   a. A voice in pupil placement so that handicapped children are with teachers who feel confident to meet their needs.

   b. Fewer children in their classrooms, or the assistance of teacher aides.

   c. Continuing opportunities for inservice training, plus technical assistance with day-to-day problems.

   d. Access to special instructional materials and resources.

2. Regular classroom teachers should be able to:

   a. Describe the educational progress and needs of children in functional terms. Use expressions such as, "She does well in spelling for her age," or "She needs to learn to write complete sentences," rather than describing the children by category of exceptionality.

   b. Carry out educational assessment and needs identification.

   c. Understand the perceptual, physical, emotional, and intellectual developmental levels that are necessary for academic achievement.

   d. Help children not handicapped to accept and appreciate the contributions of their handicapped classmates.

   e. Participate with others in meeting the needs of the handicapped.

   f. Work with aides, parents, and volunteers in the classroom.

GUIDELINES FOR ITINERANT TEACHERS

1. Itinerant teachers usually work with the deaf and the visually impaired. The itinerant teacher should:

   a. Expect that regular teachers receive information from the school principal about the service.

   b. Insure that time is provided for consultation with classroom teachers.

c. Be provided with assessment results and other diagnostic and prescriptive information. (The itinerant teacher may be the one assessing students in the area of her expertise.)
d. Work with classroom teachers in setting schedules.
e. Evaluate a student's progress at least weekly. The evaluation should indicate that the IEP is being implemented.

Our final suggestion on mainstreaming involves all the persons mentioned above: No matter how successful the integration program appears, if the subject matter presented is not appropriate to the needs of the students, we are still depriving these young people of a suitable education. The following observations point this out:

> A teacher of English literature individualizes a course on literary appreciation to fit every pupil in the room, but the question arises if this is an appropriate use of time for a mentally retarded student programmed into the class. We cannot lose sight of the fact that retarded individuals have a significant academic disability, that it takes them a long time to assimilate knowledge; therefore, courses in the liberal arts are generally bypassed by these students for the more practical subjects.

> In another situation, an observant teacher is concerned about maintaining a curriculum of practical skills needed by the handicapped. She states, "The ability to perform such jobs as sweeping, busing dishes, and doing simple assembly work requires specific practice and training for many special education students. They should have classes in which they're taught these things. If regular education doesn't provide for this, special education must accept the responsibility."

Summary

In a classroom which satisfactorily integrates the handicapped, (1) the social climate is conducive to interaction among all students, (2) instruction is individualized, (3) an evaluation system is in operation that lends itself to reporting to parents and others, and (4) the subjects taught are appropriate to the educational needs of the students.

Chapter Eleven

PL 94-142 and the
Individualized Education Program

Planning not only reduces the time required for execution, but it also provides improved results.

The IEP, mandated for special education under PL 94-142, dramatically alters the traditional lockstep system of education still practiced to a great extent in regular education. In the IEP operation, a student compares his achievement with his goals — goals set with his ability, course background, and learning modality in mind. Teachers know progress is made when the student advances toward his individualized objectives, not when he advances in comparison to other students in the room.

What Is an
Individualized Education Program?

The term "individualized education program" means a written statement of an education program for each handicapped child.

1. The IEP must state:
   a. The child's present levels of educational performance.
   b. Annual goals and short term instructional objectives.
   c. Specific special education and related services to be provided.

    d. The extent the child will participate in regular educational programs.

    e. The projected dates for initiation of services, and their anticipated duration.

    f. Objective criteria and evaluation procedures for determining, on at least an annual basis, whether objectives are being achieved.

2. The IEP must be in effect:

    a. At the beginning of each school year. School districts, and other public agencies involved in the education of children, are required to have an IEP for every handicapped child they serve.

    b. Before special education and related services are provided to a child.

    c. As soon as possible following the IEP meeting. Exceptions to this would be when meetings occur during vacation, or when there is a short delay to work out transportation.

3. The law also requires districts to hold meetings at least once each year in order to review, and if appropriate to revise, each child's IEP. These meetings could be on the anniversary date of the IEP.

Four Steps in the Development of an IEP

As a district begins to conduct a successful IEP program, it must keep these factors in mind: first, the screening of students who are having problems; second, the referral of students for evaluation relative to providing them with special education; third, the actual evaluation; and finally, the drafting of the IEPs, their review, and possible revision. Now let's look at each of these more closely.

1. The Screening Process

We'll assume there's a person in charge of screening. She answers questions regarding purpose and procedures, provides screening forms, collects them, and sees that proper post-screening follow-up is done.

A point to remember here is that children identified in the

screening process are not automatically eligible for special education. Some children's problems will be resolved in the regular classroom. Others will indicate a need for special education. Screening should never imply that a student who is not functioning adequately is thereby handicapped.

A district has to determine the screening instrument it will use. Figures 11-1 and 11-2 are sample forms that are in common use.

During a meeting of the school staff a representative of special education should:

1. Explain that screening is to assist in identifying children who may need additional school support services.
2. Explain what support services are available, including special education services.
3. Give teachers a sample screening form (Figure 11-1, Figure 11-2, or Sample 1 in Appendix B) and go over it with them, answering all questions.
4. Explain that screening is not a test. It requires no response from the student, and does not require parental approval.
5. Explain that screening is for children who appear to be functioning inadequately. It's not for all children.
6. Explain that children who are screened will be given further study. Some will enter special education; others will have their problems resolved in other ways.
7. Explain that screening forms should be used by teachers, principals, counselors, and all other professional personnel.

School districts find it helpful to inform parents of the district's concern about their child's progress at the time of screening. Parent interviews are encouraged, although the legal requirement to inform parents of the school's concern doesn't occur until the district proposes to administer individual tests and needs written parental consent.

Recall that, in addition to school people, parents, physicians, and other appropriate persons can also refer a student for special education. When this occurs, teachers involved with the student should fill out a screening form. For children who have not been in school, screening information is gathered from external sources.

Figure 11-1
SCREENING/RECORD REVIEW
ELEMENTARY FORM

Student _____Birthdate _____Sex _____Grade _____

Teacher _____School _____District _____

Is the child currently receiving Special Education Services: Yes ( )   No ( ) If Yes, describe ____

Teachers are requested to mark this screening inventory for each child who, in their opinion, appears to be functioning inadequately because of apparent exceptional mental, emotional, or physical condition(s).

Please check the statements which you think apply to this child. If the statement does not apply, do not mark it. If a specific descriptor applies to the child, underline it. Add descriptors if necessary.

The following problems exist

Date _____

To be completed by teacher, principal, or counselor after the record review has been completed.

DESCRIBE OR
SUMMARIZE:
COMMUNICATION
PROBLEMS

	sometimes	often	always	
COMMUNICATION PROBLEMS				
Expressive language (problems in syntax, grammar, limited vocabulary)	( )	( )	( )	
Receptive language (comprehension, not following directions, poor concept development)	( )	( )	( )	
Speech (poor enunciation, lisps, stutters, infantile speech, omits sounds from words, adds sound to words, substitutes sounds, unpleasant or odd voice)	( )	( )	( )	
Other (describe) _____ _____	( )	( )	( )	

				PHYSICAL PROBLEMS
PHYSICAL PROBLEMS				
Physical defect (lame, paralysis, deformity)	( )	( )	( )	
Erratic muscle movements	( )	( )	( )	
Gross motor coordination (awkward, clumsy, poor balance)	( )	( )	( )	
Fine motor coordination (eye-hand, manual dexterity)	( )	( )	( )	
Visual (cannot see blackboard, squints, rubs eyes, holds book too close, eyes oscillate involuntarily, cross-eyed)	( )	( )	( )	

Figure 11-1 (continued)

	The following problems exist		
	sometimes	often	always
Hearing (unable to discriminate sounds, asks to have instructions repeated, turns ear to speaker, strains to hear, often has earaches)	( )	( )	( )
Not toilet trained	( )	( )	( )
Unusually small (at least 20% less than class average)	( )	( )	( )
Unusually overweight (at least 20% more than class average)	( )	( )	( )
Other (describe, e.g., epilepsy, circulatory problems, dental problems, respiratory problems)	( )	( )	( )

DIRECTIONS: Please complete by reviewing all existing school records, including the health card. To be completed by designated procedures.

STANDARDIZED TEST INFORMATION (last three years)

Test Name	Date Given	Grade and Age When Tested	Standard Score	G.E.	Percentile
_____	_____	_____	_____	_____	_____
_____	_____	_____	_____	_____	_____
_____	_____	_____	_____	_____	_____
_____	_____	_____	_____	_____	_____
_____	_____	_____	_____	_____	_____
_____	_____	_____	_____	_____	_____
_____	_____	_____	_____	_____	_____
_____	_____	_____	_____	_____	_____

COLLATERAL SCHOLASTIC INFORMATION

1) Record of Retention   No ( )   Yes ( ), grades retained _____year(s) _____
2) Record of Skipping   No ( )   Yes ( ), grades placed _____year(s) _____
   (Skipping a Grade)

CURRENT SERVICE INFORMATION

1) Speech Therapy   No ( )   Yes ( ) If Yes, describe _____
2) Physical/Medical Program   No ( )   Yes ( ) If Yes, describe _____

Figure 11-1 (continued)

REVIEW OF PHYSICAL HISTORY

1. Past Medical Problems: Yes ( ), specify _____
2. Current Medical Problems: Yes ( ), specify _____
3. Past Medications Administered: Yes ( ), specify _____
4. Current Medications Administered: Yes ( ), specify _____
5. Past Physical Disabilities: Yes ( ), specify _____
6. Current Physical Disabilities: Yes ( ), specify _____
7. Past Vision Problems: Yes ( ) Current Problems: No ( )   Yes ( )
8. Past Hearing Problems: Yes ( ) Current Problems: No ( )   Yes ( )
9. Past Speech Problems: Yes ( ) Current Problems: No ( )   Yes ( )
10. Past Perceptual Problems: Yes ( ) Current Problems: No ( )   Yes ( )
11. Coordination Problems: Fine Motor Yes ( ): specify _____

    Gross Motor Yes ( ): specify _____

CLASSROOM BEHAVIOR PROBLEMS	These problems occur in the classroom as often as:			DESCRIBE OR SUMMARIZE CLASSROOM BEHAVIOR PROBLEMS
	15-25%	26-50%	Over 50%	
Overly energetic, talks out, out of seat	( )	( )	( )	
Very quiet, uncommunicative	( )	( )	( )	
Acting Out (aggressive, hostile, rebellious, destructive)	( )	( )	( )	
Cries easily, explosive	( )	( )	( )	
Inattentive (short attention span, doesn't stick to task, fails to complete tasks)	( )	( )	( )	
Doesn't appear to notice what is happening in the immediate environment	( )	( )	( )	
Poor peer relationships (few friends, rejected, ignored, abused by peers)	( )	( )	( )	
Other (describe) _____ _____	( )	( )	( )	

Figure 11-1 (continued)

ACADEMIC PROBLEMS	Performance is below average class level as often as:			ACADEMIC PROBLEMS
	15-25%	26-50%	Over 50%	
Reading				
Word attack skills	( )	( )	( )	
Reverses, substitutes	( )	( )	( )	
Oral reading	( )	( )	( )	
Silent reading	( )	( )	( )	
Comprehension	( )	( )	( )	
Other _____	( )	( )	( )	
Writing (illegible, reverses letters, doesn't write)	( )	( )	( )	
Mathematics				
Basic computation	( )	( )	( )	
Concepts	( )	( )	( )	
Set operations	( )	( )	( )	
Verbal problems	( )	( )	( )	
Other _____	( )	( )	( )	
Spelling (cannot spell phonetically, omits or adds letters)	( )	( )	( )	
Social Sciences, Sciences (doesn't handle concepts, doesn't understand relationships, poor understanding of cause and effect)	( )	( )	( )	
Other (describe) _____				
_____	( )	( )	( )	

Date _____

(Signature of person completing form)

Figure 11-1 (continued)

To be completed by teacher, counselor or principal

Date: _____

DESCRIPTION OF CURRENT PROGRAM OBJECTIVES

If no referral is being made or while the referral is being processed, what is being done by the school to remediate the problem:

Nature of recommended referral:

Figure 11-2
SCREENING/RECORD REVIEW
SECONDARY FORM

Student _____Birthdate _____Sex _____Grade _____

Teacher _____School _____District _____

Is the child currently receiving Special Education Services: Yes ( ) No ( ) If Yes, describe ____

_____

Teachers are requested to mark this screening inventory for each child who, in their opinion, appears to be functioning inadequately because of apparent exceptional mental, emotional, or physical condition(s).

Please check the statements which you think apply to this child. If the statement does not apply, do not mark it. If a specific descriptor applies to the child, underline it. Add descriptors if necessary.

Date _____

To be completed by teacher, principal, or counselor after the record review has been completed.

The following problems exist

COMMUNICATION PROBLEMS	sometimes	often	always
Expressive language (problems in syntax, grammar, limited vocabulary)	( )	( )	( )
Receptive language (comprehension, not following directions, poor concept development)	( )	( )	( )
Speech (poor enunciation, lisps, stutters, infantile speech, omits sounds from words, adds sound to words, substitutes sounds, unpleasant or odd voice)	( )	( )	( )
Other (describe) _____ _____	( )	( )	( )

DESCRIBE OR SUMMARIZE COMMUNICATION PROBLEMS

PHYSICAL PROBLEMS			
Physical defect (lame, paralysis, deformity)	( )	( )	( )
Erratic muscle movements	( )	( )	( )
Gross motor coordination (awkward, clumsy, poor balance)	( )	( )	( )
Fine motor coordination (eye-hand, manual dexterity)	( )	( )	( )
Visual (cannot see blackboard, squints, rubs eyes, holds book too close, eyes oscillate involuntarily, cross-eyed)	( )	( )	( )

PHYSICAL PROBLEMS

Figure 11-2 (continued)

	The following problems exist		
	sometimes	often	always
Hearing (unable to discriminate sounds, asks to have instructions repeated, turns ear to speaker, strains to hear, often has earaches)	( )	( )	( )
Lack of personal hygiene	( )	( )	( )
Unusually small (at least 20% less than class average)	( )	( )	( )
Unusually overweight (at least 20% more than class average)	( )	( )	( )
Other (describe, e.g., epilepsy, circulatory problems, dental problems, respiratory problems)	( )	( )	( )

DIRECTIONS: Please complete by reviewing all existing school records, including the health card. To be completed by designated procedures.

STANDARDIZED TEST INFORMATION (last three years)

Test Name	Date Given	Grade and Age When Tested	Standard Score	G.E.	Percentile
____	____	____	____	____	____
____	____	____	____	____	____
____	____	____	____	____	____
____	____	____	____	____	____
____	____	____	____	____	____
____	____	____	____	____	____
____	____	____	____	____	____

COLLATERAL SCHOLASTIC INFORMATION

1) Record of Retention   No ( )   Yes ( ), grades retained _____year(s) _____

2) Record of Skipping   No ( )   Yes ( ), grades placed _____year(s) _____
   (Skipping a Grade)

CURRENT SERVICE INFORMATION

1) Speech Therapy   No ( )   Yes ( ) If Yes, describe _____

2) Physical/Medical Program No ( )   Yes ( ) If Yes, describe _____

3) In Special Education   No ( )   Yes ( ) If Yes, describe _____

Figure 11-2 (continued)

REVIEW OF PHYSICAL HISTORY

1. Past Medical Problems: Yes ( ), specify _____
2. Current Medical Problems: Yes ( ), specify _____
3. Past Medications Administered: Yes ( ), specify _____
4. Current Medications Administered: Yes ( ), specify _____
5. Past Physical Disabilities: Yes ( ), specify _____
6. Current Physical Disabilities: Yes ( ), specify _____
7. Past Vision Problems: Yes ( ) Current Problems: No ( )   Yes ( )
8. Past Hearing Problems: Yes ( ) Current Problems: No ( )   Yes ( )
9. Past Speech Problems: Yes ( ) Current Problems: No ( )   Yes ( )
10. Past Perceptual Problems: Yes ( ) Current Problems: No ( )   Yes ( )
11. Coordination Problems: Fine Motor Yes ( ): specify _____
    Gross Motor Yes ( ): specify _____

CLASSROOM BEHAVIOR PROBLEMS	These problems occur in the classroom as often as:			DESCRIBE OR SUMMARIZE: CLASSROOM BEHAVIOR PROBLEMS
	15-25%	26-50%	Over 50%	
Overly energetic, talks out, out of seat	( )	( )	( )	
Very quiet, uncommunicative	( )	( )	( )	
Acting Out (aggressive, hostile, rebellious, destructive)	( )	( )	( )	
Cries easily, explosive	( )	( )	( )	
Inattentive (short attention span, doesn't stick to task, fails to complete tasks)	( )	( )	( )	
Doesn't appear to notice what is happening in the immediate environment	( )	( )	( )	
Poor peer relationships (few friends, rejected, ignored, abused by peers)	( )	( )	( )	
Not in attendance				
Other (describe) _____				
_____				
_____	( )	( )	( )	

Figure 11-2 (continued)

ACADEMIC PROBLEMS	Performance is below average class level as often as:			ACADEMIC PROBLEMS
	15-25%	26-50%	Over 50%	
Reading				
Retaining	( )	( )	( )	
Comprehension	( )	( )	( )	
Other _____	( )	( )	( )	
Writing (illegible, reverses letters, doesn't write)	( )	( )	( )	
Mathematics				
Basic computation	( )	( )	( )	
Concepts	( )	( )	( )	
Other _____	( )	( )	( )	
Spelling (cannot spell phonetically, omits or adds letters)	( )	( )	( )	
Social Sciences, Sciences (doesn't handle concepts, doesn't understand relationships, poor understanding of cause and effect)	( )	( )	( )	
Other (describe) _____				
_____	( )	( )	( )	

Date _____

(Signature of person completing form)

Figure 11-2 (continued)

To be completed by teacher, counselor or principal

Date: _____

DESCRIPTION OF CURRENT PROGRAM OBJECTIVES

If no referral is being made or while the referral is being processed, what is being done by the school to remediate the problem:

Nature of recommended referral:

2. The Referral Process

All screening forms are given to the referral committee. This group could be composed of your standing IEP team, or any other group already organized. We have separated the committees here to point out more clearly the individual steps.

The referral people examine the screening forms and process them as necessary, being careful to follow confidentiality procedures. They select and notify those who will do the evaluation, and see that the evaluators have the appropriate information. Every child who is screened is referred for some degree of evaluation. The decision as to who enters special education comes after all evaluation reports are in and a meeting of the evaluation team is called.

3. The Evaluation Process

Evaluators comprise such professionals as teachers, medical doctors, psychometrists, and psychiatrists. These people don't necessarily meet as a group; so it is necessary that one person coordinate this many-faceted task. The material which follows describes what must be done.

The first order of business is to get written parental consent for the evaluation. Figure 11-3 is a sample form to obtain this permission.

Assuming that parental permission is obtained, there are other federal requirements we should review. Your district should insure that:

1. Tests and other evaluation instruments:
    a. Are administered in the child's native language, or other adaptive modes of communication, when that is best for the child.
    b. Have been validated for the specific purpose for which they are used.
    c. Are recommended by their producer for the purpose for which they are used.
    d. Are administered by persons who meet certification or licensure requirements under your state law.
2. Tests are used that assess specific areas of educational need.
3. Tests reflect aptitude or achievement level, rather than the child's impaired sensory, manual, or speaking skills. (Except where those skills are the factors which the test purports to measure.)

Figure 11-3
SAMPLE PARENTAL CONSENT
FORM LETTER

Date _____

Dear _____:

This letter concerns your child _____, bd. _____

From our former communication, you are aware of our concern for your child's educational progress and the need to gather information so that the best possible program can be planned. Regulations require that you give written consent for any testing or other evaluation of your child before we may proceed. Please read the following material, and check and sign as indicated on the form below. Detach on the dotted line and send, or bring, the form to my office. If you have any questions, please don't hesitate to call. Your cooperation is appreciated.

HERE ARE THE TESTS TO BE USED WHEN EVALUATING YOUR CHILD:

Intelligence: _____
          Description of test(s)

Communication: _____
          Description of test(s)

Physical: _____
          Description of test(s)

Behavior: _____
          Description of test(s)

Academic: _____
          Description of test(s)

Other: _____
          Description of test(s)

Before granting permission for an evaluation of your child, it is important that you be aware of and understand the following:

1. You have the right to review all records related to the referral.
2. You have the right to refuse to permit the evaluation.
3. You have the right to be fully informed of the results of the evaluation.
4. If you disagree with the results, you have the right to get an outside evaluation.
5. You have a right to review the instruments (tests) used to evaluate your child.

Sincerely yours,

_____
Director of Special Education

. . . .

Figure 11-3 (continued)

Date _____

This is to indicate that I have been informed regarding the referral of my child _____
_____for individual testing or other evaluation, using appropriate assessment instruments.

☐ Permission is given to conduct the evaluation as described.
☐ Permission is not given to conduct the evaluation.
☐ Request conference prior to granting permission.

_____
Parent's Signature

_____
Date

4. No one test, or type of test, is used as the sole criterion for placement.

5. Information is gathered concerning the child's physical condition, socio-cultural background, and adaptive behavior in home and school.

6. The interpretation of the data is made by persons knowledgeable about the evaluation.

7. The evaluation includes:

   a. The student's current level of educational functioning, his weaknesses, strengths, and areas in need of support intervention.

   b. Statements describing expected achievement during the current academic year. At the IEP meeting these will be restated as short and long term goals.

   c. What educational setting best meets the needs of the child.

   d. What physical, mental, and emotional impairments affect the child's educational potential, and what steps should be taken to alleviate the problem.

Closely following a student's evaluation, the person in charge of this procedure calls a meeting of those involved to determine whether the results warrant the child being declared eligible for special education. If it's obvious that the student is eligible, this meeting can be the IEP meeting.

4. The Drafting of the Individualized Education Program (IEP)

The standing IEP committee, plus other appropriate participants, meet to formulate a student's individualized education program within 30 days of the date he is declared eligible for special education. Regulations accompanying PL 94-142 state that the committee must be composed of at least the following persons:

   a. A representative of the school, other than the child's teacher, who is qualified to provide, or supervise, special education.

   b. The child's teacher.

   c. One or both parents, .

   d. The child, where appropriate.

e. Other individuals at the discretion of parent or school.

f. A person knowledgeable about the evaluation and its results must attend the meeting for a child who has been evaluated for the first time.

The chairperson of the IEP team can be one of the school people mentioned above. It is this person's responsibility to:

1. Gather all evaluation material and have it available at the IEP meeting.

2. Notify participants of the meeting and set a time and place mutually agreeable to parents and school people.

3. Document efforts to involve parents in their child's IEP meeting.

4. Preside at the meeting.

5. Keep an on-going record of the meeting. For example, as the short term goals are decided, the chairperson writes them down on the proper form. (See Figure 11-4).

6. Obtain parent's signature for placement of his child in a special education program. (Recall that it is not obligatory to have parents' signature on the IEP form, unless the IEP form is combined with the parent permission-for-placement form.)

7. See that copies of the IEP are distributed to the teachers involved, placed in the student's folder, and available to parents upon request.

8. See that the IEP is reviewed on or before the anniversary date. Also see that a thorough reassessment is done every three years.

In deciding which teachers will participate in the meetings, the administrator of special education considers the following:

1. For a child already in special education, the "teacher" could be the child's special education teacher.

2. For a student being considered for special education, the "teacher" could be the child's regular teacher, or one qualified to provide special education.

3. If the child is not in school, or has more than one teacher, the school and special education administration agree on who will participate as the teacher.

In the above material we've mentioned chairpersons of the various committees. Some districts go about this another way. They appoint IEP case-workers who take on a number of cases (students identified from screening procedures as needing specail education) and carry them through all the steps.

Parents and the IEP

Parental involvement in the development of the child's IEP is important:

1. Information a parent brings to the committee enriches the understanding of the child and his family.
2. Involvement usually is associated with a greater degree of parent/teacher cooperation.
3. The parent's presence helps his understanding of special education.

In addition, regulations under PL 94-142 require the following:

1. Each district shall take steps to insure that one or both parents are present at the IEP meeting.
2. Notice of the meeting must indicate the purpose, time, location, and persons attending. (See Figure 11-5.)
3. A meeting may be conducted without a parent in attendance. In this case the district must record its attempts to arrange an agreed upon time and place. Examples:
    a. Detailed records of telephone calls.
    b. Copies of correspondence.
    c. Detailed records of home visits.
4. The district shall take whatever action necessary to insure that parents understand the proceedings at the meeting. For example, it may be necessary to have an interpreter for the deaf, or for those whose language is other than English.
5. The district shall give the parent, on request, a copy of the child's individualized education program.

A sample letter inviting parents to an IEP meeting is provided in Figure 11-5.

Figure 11-4
SAMPLE IEP FORM

☐ Initial Placement
INDIVIDUALIZED EDUCATION PROGRAM   ☐ Annual Review

CHILD'S NAME _____BIRTHDATE _____

ADDRESS _____.PHONE _____

DISTRICT OF RESIDENCY _____DATE OF MEETING _____

In attendance at IEP meeting: _____
                 Name   Position

_____   _____   _____

Name, Position   Name, Position   Name, Position

Special Education Information:

1. Entry Date _____   2. Review Date _____

3 Child's Teachers (1) _____ (2) _____
                 Teacher, Subject   Teacher, Subject

    (3) _____
      Teacher, Subject

4. (See following page(s) for statement of current level of educational functioning, long term objectives, short term objectives, and instructional strategies.)

5. Is special physical education programming required?   Yes ☐   No ☐

    Describe Program:

6. Related Services:

    Speech Therapy (describe) _____

    Physical Therapy (describe) _____

    Occupational Therapy (describe) _____

    Work Experience (describe) _____

    Medical Service (excluding treatment) (describe) _____

_____

    Social Services (describe) _____

    Transportation (describe) _____

    Other (describe) _____

_____

7. Describe the ways (programs, classes) the child will participate in the regular program; include an estimate of the extent of time the child will be in these regular classes and programs.

Figure 11-4 (continued)

- -

Parent Consent-for-Placement

I understand my child, ————————————, bd, —————————, has been evaluated and is found to be in need of special education services because of a handicapping condition which, at this time, is diagnosed as (type of handicap) ————— ——————. In addition, I have participated in the development of my child's individualized education program and have had his/her program and the related services which are available to him/her explained to me. I approve of my child's placement in special education.

Parent's Signature	Date

Figure 11-4 (continued)

INDIVIDUAL IMPLEMENTATION PLAN (IEP continued)

(Complete as many forms as required, one for each area
where the student will receive special education.)

Student's Name _____ Birthdate _____

(Consideration is given to academic potential and background, social adaptation, and pre-vocational/vocational, psychomotor, and self-help skills
that are pertinent to the area stated below.)

AREA _____ Current Level of Educational Functioning (include strengths and weaknesses)

Long Term Objectives (Annual Goals)	Short Term Objectives	Strategies (To be completed by teacher)	Materials	Start (Date)	Complete (Date)

Least Restrictive Instructional Environment:	Procedures for Evaluating Progress Toward Achieving Short Term Objectives:

164

Figure 11-5

Date _____

Dear _____:

In order for an individualized education program to be effective for a child it is important that school people and parents work together as a team.

As you know, we have been completing an evaluation of _____. We would like to meet with you to share this information. At this meeting you will have the opportunity, along with other team members, to assist in the development of an education program for your child.

The meeting will be on (date) _____ at (time) _____ in (location) _____. Persons attending the meeting are _____ (position); _____ (position); _____ (position); and yourself.

If you are unable to attend the meeting, please contact us at (phone) _____so we can plan a time which is mutually convenient.

Your cooperation is greatly appreciated.

Sincerely,

_____, _____
(name)   (position)

Format for an IEP

A sample IEP form is given in Figure 11-4. It can be used during staff meetings and inservice courses to clarify the purpose and procedures of the IEP. We also suggest that a copy be given to all participants at an IEP meeting. The chairperson, of course, uses it to record the meeting.

As you can see by the form, we feel that the IEP meeting is a good time for parents to sign the consent-for-placement statement. It appears in Figure 11-4 below the dotted line. We also ask you to note that Figure 11-4 has a space to enter the child's particular handicap (mentally retarded, learning disabled, etc.). We suggest that prior to making copies of the IEP to give to teachers, this part (below the dotted line) be cut off. This precaution relieves teachers of unnecessary concern regarding confidentiality. The complete form, of course, should be securely filed in a prearranged place.

The administrator of special education should be aware that the "statement of the particular handicap" on the consent-for-placement form in Figure 11-4 is just a suggestion. The law doesn't say that consent-for-placement must include the category of handicap. However, PL 94-142, in defining "consent," includes the following: "The parent has been fully informed of all information relevant to the activity for which consent is sought...." The term "all information" would surely seem to include the handicapping condition. Also, the type of handicap is clearly one of the results obtained from the evaluation. To withhold this information from parents may be a breach of the law's intent.

Another reason why it's good policy to include the handicapping condition is related to the use your district makes of the information. During the federally required census, your district counts the number of handicapped children it serves by category of handicap; so many mentally retarded, so many seriously emotionally disturbed, and so on. Now, if a parent were to ask, "Is my child one of the ones you count as mentally retarded?" and the answer is "Yes," what explanation could be offered for failure to tell him this at the time you presumably shared with him the full results of his child's evaluation?

Naturally, this information won't be belabored. It usually serves no practical purpose except for the aforementioned census report, and perhaps as information parents should be aware of in order to apply for supplemental social security for their child.

Tips on Getting Parental Consent

One of the things you'll have to decide is whether to go ahead with an IEP meeting before you have parental consent for placement, or to work on the consent problem and only when it is resolved convene the IEP team. Let's examine the possibilities:

1. Parents who attend IEP meetings almost always give written consent for placement at that time. So if you're sure a parent will participate, you'll go ahead and have the meeting.

2. Parents who state they're not going to consent to placement but will attend the meeting are open for convincing. You'll probably go ahead with the meeting.

3. Parents who will neither give consent nor attend the meeting need more counseling. No use setting up an IEP for their child at this time.

4. Finally, you have the case where you thought the parent was coming but didn't appear. You have the meeting but how do you handle the results? Figure 11-6 presents one method that works for a number of districts. (The "results" of the IEP meeting referred to in the letter in this Figure are the items presented in Figure 11-4. A completed copy should be enclosed with the letter. With one exception: that part of Figure 11-4 titled "Parent Consent-for-Placement" should be taken out. There's a section in Figure 11-6 for parent consent.)

If this form is mailed, we suggest it be sent by registered mail because of the confidential information specifying the child's handicap. The responsibility for getting the parent's signature on the form can be given to the chairperson of the IEP team. The child cannot be placed in a special education program under PL 94-142 unless the parent has given written permission.

There's one more item to be mentioned here. It concerns procedural safeguards. To insure that they have informed parents of their rights, many districts enclose Figure 11-7 with all parental communications. This saves time in sorting out which safeguard explanations go with the request for evaluation, which go with

Figure 11-6
SAMPLE COMMUNICATION REGARDING
IEP MEETING RESULTS AND
PARENT CONSENT-FOR-PLACEMENT

Dear _____ :   Date _____

As you know, a meeting was held on _____to develop an appropriate individualized education program for your child. We are enclosing a copy of the results of that meeting, and also a form asking for your permission to place your child in special education. The recent evaluation of your child, which we did with your consent, shows that _____ _____ is in need of special education services because of a handicapping condition which, at this time, is diagnosed as (type of handicap) _____ .

It is important that you understand that: (a) your child's placement in special education is considered to be appropriate and beneficial at this time, (b) you have a right to refuse consent to your child's placement, and (c) you will be invited to attend meetings to review your child's progress and continued placement on an annual basis, or whenever you and the school people feel a review is necessary.

Please review and check and sign the following consent form. Detach on the dotted line and return it to this office. If you have any questions feel free to call me at (phone) _____ .

Sincerely,

_____, _____
(Name)   (Position)

– –

   I have received copies of the suggested placement and educational program for my child _____, _____
                          (name)   (birthdate)

☐ I agree with the special education program that has been developed, and I give my consent for placement of my child in special education. I understand that no change in my child's placement will occur without prior notice, and that I have the right to refuse consent at any time.

☐ I do not agree with the special education program. I do not give my consent for placement.

☐ I request a conference concerning my child's education program.

_____   _____
(Parent's Signature)   (Date)

Figure 11-7
NOTICE TO PARENTS

Explanation of Procedural Safeguards
and Due Process

The following is an explanation of your rights according to the law. The intent is to keep you fully informed concerning decisions about your child and to inform you of your rights if you disagree with any of those decisions.

1. **Right to review all school records.**

   You have the right to see and examine all school records related to your child. The district will supply you, upon request, a list of the types and location of education records collected, maintained, or used by the district. If you feel that certain records are inaccurate or misleading, you have the right to ask that they be removed from your child's file. Copies of any material pertaining to your child will be available to you, upon request.

2. **Right to review evaluation tests and procedures.**

   You have the right to examine all tests and procedures that are used to determine if your child is in need of special education services and what these educational needs are.

3. **Right to refuse to permit evaluation(s) or a change in your child's educational placement.**

   You have the right to withhold permission for your child's educational placement either to be changed or to be tested.

4. **Right to be informed of the results of evaluation(s).**

   You have the right to have the results of all testing of your child explained to you.

5. **Right to obtain an independent evaluation.**

   If you do not feel the school's evaluation is fair or accurate, you may request an educational evaluation from an agency or professional outside the school at public expense. However, the school may request a hearing if its evaluation is challenged. If the hearing rules in favor of the school, the school does not have to pay for the independent evaluation.

6. **Right to request an impartial due process hearing.**

   If you do not agree with the school's actions at any point concerning the identification, evaluation or placement of your child, you have the right to request an impartial due process hearing. If you request a hearing:

Figure 11-7 (continued)

a. You must notify the district in writing within 20 days of receipt of a notice from the school concerning your child's identification, evaluation or placement.

b. The district shall inform you of any free or low cost legal or other relevant services available so that you may be represented at the hearing by trained counsel.

c. The hearing will be open to the public and under the authority and jurisdiction of the school district.

d. Your child may be present at the hearing if you desire.

e. Your child will remain in his/her current educational placement during pending of any administrative or judicial proceedings or, if applying for initial admission to public school, the child will be placed in school with your consent except if conduct by the child constitutes imminent danger to the health and safety of the child and others.

7. **Right to give consent or deny access to your child's educational records.**

Parental consent must be obtained before personally identifiable information is (a) disclosed to anyone other than educational personnel, or (b) used for any purpose other than that for which it was collected. It is the district's responsibility to notify you when either condition (a) or (b) occurs. The district maintains a list of those employees within the district who are authorized to have access to personally identifiable information.

In addition, the district will notify you when personally identifiable information is no longer needed to provide educational services to your child. *You have the right to request the destruction of this information.*

IEP information, and so on. The complete list of legal rights (Figure 11-7) is sent with every contact.

See Appendix B for a full assortment of sample forms.

In summary, the IEP accomplishes the following:

1. A series of statements of current and expected performance levels for specific tasks or behaviors is established in some or all of the following areas:

Language	Social
Speech	Psychomotor
Hearing	Mobility
Academic	Vocational
Non-academic	Self-help

2. Long term goals and short term goals are established.
3. Specific special education and related services to be provided are delineated. Dates for beginning and ending services are set.
4. The student is assigned to the least restrictive environment.
5. The length of time the student will spend in the regular classroom is stated.
6. Strategies are developed to assist the child in achieving his IEP goals and objectives.
7. Procedures for at least an annual evaluation of the IEP are set, including the date.
8. If a parent is at the meeting, he gives written consent for initial placement of his child in special education at this time.

Chapter Twelve

How to Get Parents Involved

Hearing is a physical process...listening is an intellectual one. Genuine listening is difficult work and requires increased energy.

Recently, a group of state education people gave an inservice to school administrators on PL 94-142. A participant asked this question: "Some parents are not interested in taking part in their child's IEP, or in what education program we put the child. Are we allowed to place the child if the parents flatly refuse to be involved?"

The response was a direct quotation from the regulations under PL 94-142: "The district shall not place a child in a special educational program without written parental consent. If the district wishes to place a child in a special education program and is unable to obtain written parental consent, the district may request a hearing on the matter. The hearing officer's decision is binding on all parties subject to a review of the hearing by the Chief State School Officer upon request, and subject to court action."

This is a fair, clear answer to a question, but a complete response might have indicated some methods that work in getting parents interested in their child's education. In other words, the next question could be:

What Hampers Parents from Becoming Involved?

Schools have a long history of placing children in whatever program they see fit without parental involvement. Thus, a parent isn't used to being part of the education planning and feels awkward in his new role. Even when school people welcome the parent into the educational conference — and many of them do — they aren't too sure, themselves, of the part he should play. A clearly conceptualized role of a parent's involvement in his child's public school education has yet to be developed.

Another inhibiting factor is the apprehension of some teachers and school administrators when parents are actively engaged at the decision-making level. It was all right to meet parents at the tea table during parent-teacher meetings, or to inform them of their child's progress during a parent conference, or even to have them visit the classroom from time to time. But the new, powerful role of parents in education will take time, training, and intelligent planning in order to make it a good experience for all. Our task is to explore the most beneficial ways to involve parents, and then to work with them once they become actively engaged.

Listen to Parents, Don't Just Hear Them

Not long ago, I was privileged to be on a committee composed of parents and other advocates for handicapped children, whose purpose was to develop a set of guidelines for parent monitoring. Listen to some of the things parents said during our meetings:

"When I go into a room I get a gut feeling about the teacher. I can tell if she likes children or not."

"I can spend five minutes talking with a teacher and get a positive or negative feeling."

One mother put it this way: "Parents have to get a good feeling when they're in the classroom; otherwise they'll never think the teacher is doing very much."

Another woman asked if other parents thought about their children's attitude. "Maybe the kids just don't like the teacher," she said, "and they set the tone of the classroom."

The response came quickly from a vocal mother: "The teacher's attitude is more important than the students'. Teachers guide the children, not the other way around."

"That's right," another parent volunteered, "It's the teacher who makes the atmosphere."

A parent who had apparently done quite a bit of visiting in her son's classroom summarized her feelings this way: "When I go into a classroom where my son is I check out if the teacher is following his program. I also watch how the teacher handles the whole room. Classroom management and discipline are really important. The next thing I look at is how the teacher teaches. How, exactly, does she help my child learn a new skill in reading?"

"You're probably thinking about the new thing called the IEP," another mother responded. "Well, I've asked for a copy of my kid's IEP, but so far they've put me off. I haven't gotten one."

"That's exactly why we're here," someone else put in. "We have to set up questions that can't be ignored. If the laws says the kids have to have IEPs, then we have a right to have proof that our kids have them."

"Believe me, I'm going to do something about my boy's IEP," a very concerned parent offered. "Since September his IEP says he's to be taught Driver's Training. You know, the driver's manual so he can pass his written test. And so far no one has done a thing about it. I've called his teacher a few times and she says she's going to get at it right away. Here it is after Christmas, and he graduates in June. He doesn't have much time left. I'm going over to ＿＿＿＿＿＿ High School tomorrow, and believe me, they'd better get going on teaching him what they said they would or I'll know the reason why."

The talk about the IEPs went on for quite a while, until a young mother of a Down's Syndrome child changed the subject by saying, "You know, they always say we shouldn't talk to the teacher when we visit a classroom, but I think we should talk to the teacher. My little girl's teacher is warm and friendly. When I go into the room she always comes over and makes me welcome. Once I went in a room where the teacher acted as if I wasn't there. That gave me a funny feeling about her and the whole room."

This interchange continued for the better part of an hour. Since the committee meetings were set up to be only an hour and a-half at a stretch, the group summarized their discussion in the 30 minutes remaining. Subsequent meetings were much more precise in their development of monitoring procedures that can be utilized by parents; but this first meeting produced the following ideas, which obviously demonstrate that when parents think of their school age children, they automatically think of how the children are accepted by their teacher and their school — first and foremost.

This is the summary of the first meeting concerned with the development of a monitoring procedure for parents: First priority item — Atmosphere in the Classroom:

1. Is the teacher a warm person?
2. Is she treating the children on their level, or as babies?
3. Is she friendly with the children and visitors?
4. Are the children friendly among themselves?
5. Is the whole school receptive to handicapped children, and to visits by parents of handicapped children?

The parents we have quoted in the above paragraphs should be listened to. They are concerned enough to get together to develop a system for monitoring handicapped children's programs that will be used by many parents other than themselves. Their influence is strong.

How to Tell Parents About Their Rights

From the time a child is first suspected of being handicapped until he reaches his twenty-second birthday, it's a parent's right to be engaged in his child's education. What's more, the district has the responsibility of informing parents of this right. The old saying, "Ignorance of the law is no excuse," is true here — but with a slight twist. The district, not the parents, is to blame if parents are ignorant of the law in this regard. You must tell parents they have rights, and then inform them of what the rights consist.

One of the best ways to tell parents about their rights in general is to invite them to a parent-teacher meeting. The flyer sent home annoucing the meeting, with your name on the program, can include some basic facts about parents' rights—just enough to whet the parents' interest so you'll have a good turnout.

But the PTA meeting won't be enough. Large groups assimilate large ideas. The many and varied parts of parents' rights under PL 94-142 need careful explaining. So the meetings with parents of children receiving, or about to receive, special education should probably be limited in number, although you won't close the meeting to anyone who wants to attend. If a few, say eight or ten, correctly understand their rights under PL 94-142 and take action when necessary, they'll be examples to illustrate what you mean by parents' rights when you discuss the law with subsequent groups. In the long run, no parent of a handicapped child should be left without receiving an invitation to at least one meeting where you explain rights and answer questions.

During the meetings, it's important to talk with parents in language they understand. We, in education, have developed so much professional lingo that sometimes people not in the field find it hard to follow us. Following is an outline of ideas you'll want to discuss. It can be developed into leaflet form and passed out to parents at the meeting.

Guidelines You Can Share with Parents

If you think your child has special needs:

1. Get in touch with your nearest public school right away. If you don't get help there, go to your local superintendent of schools. Your school system is obligated by law to locate all handicapped children and provide an appropriate education for them during their school years.

2. Ask that your child be given an evaluation to find out what kind of program he should have. If the evaluation indicates he is eligible for special education, a meeting to prepare an individualized education program for him must be held within 30 days.

3. Don't forget that this applies not only to young children, but also to your high school age children with physical, mental, and emotional problems. Sometimes we spend so much time with very young children that the youth population becomes a forgotten group.

4. Find out about preschool services for your handicapped child. The principal of your neighborhood school can tell you if there are available programs in your district.

5. If your child is already in school and is having problems, make every effort to work with his teacher. Some problems can be worked out by you and the teacher and your child together. If problems persist, go ahead and ask for a thorough evaluation. Your child's teacher, counselor, or principal may carry the ball on this. But if they don't, act on your own.

6. Another important point is that you can ask for a re-evaluation of your child even if he is already in a special education program. This is especially important if you feel the placement is based on old, inaccurate, or incomplete tests, or if you are dissatisfied with your child's present program.

7. Observe how your child is getting along in his schoolwork and decide when you think he is ready for a change — a change that will place him in special education, remove him from special education, or upgrade his present curriculum regardless of the program he is in. In any of these cases, don't hesitate to request an evaluation or re-evaluation of your child. Put your request for this service in writing and send it to the school principal or district superintendent.

8. Remember, the school must ask for your written permission to test your child on an individual basis. This is necessary even if you have requested the evaluation. An explanation of all your rights should be included in the notice asking for permission (for example, your right to inspect and review all your child's school records).

9. If the school people turn down your request for evaluation, they must send you notice of this decision and explain why they have turned you down. If you wish to protest this decision, you can request a due process hearing. Your school must provide you with information on how to go ahead with the due process.

The above items are of general information for all parents. The following material pertains to children already known to be, or suspected of being, handicapped.

When Parents Ask for an Evaluation of Their Child

There are two ways the evaluation can be processed. Both of them are covered under PL 94-142, and the way a district will go depends to a great extent on the parent of the child in question.

First, the usual way is for the school to carry out the evaluation after the parent gives written permission. However, should the parent not be satisfied with the district's results, he can ask for an outside evaluation at the expense of the school district. This is the second way. If the district feels its evaluation was adequate, it can initiate a due process hearing to demonstrate that its evaluation was indeed adequate. If the hearings officer decides against the school district, the district has to pay for an outside evaluation of the child. If the decision is in favor of the school district, then the parent must either pay for the outside evaluation or abide by the evaluation results as obtained by the district — unless, of course, the parent decides to appeal further.

As a matter of practice, school districts usually do not enter any objection to the parent's request for an outside evaluation of their child. They allow it, and pay for it. In many cases it corroborates what has been found in the district's evaluation. It should be remembered that the outside evaluation has to be done by an agency or individuals agreed upon by both the school and the parent.

Here are some facts about testing and evaluation that your parents should be aware of:

1. Be satisfied that the evaluation of your child is complete. It shouldn't consist of a single test or type of test (for example, the IQ test). The results should let you know how your child is doing in all areas of his intellectual, physical, and emotional development.

2. A thorough evaluation of your child should include a physical examination. There are reasons for this. Sometimes a child is suspected of being mentally retarded when, in effect, his retardation is not mental, but caused by impaired hearing, poor eyesight, or serious anemia. Another reason: If a deaf child doesn't do well in school, don't lay it to his deafness and let it go at that. He may have undetected health problems. An accompanying health impairment is no stranger to children with other disabilities.

3. As a parent, your input to the evaluation team is important. You can inform about how your child acts round-the-clock; how he likes to learn about things, how he adapts to various social situations, and how he sees himself as a person.

4. Before you give written permission for the evaluation, ask about the tests your child will be given. Ask why each test is given, and what will be done as a result of the test. If you don't understand the answers to your questions, tell the person you're talking to. Perhaps you can ask the question in another way.

5. The tests should not discriminate against your child in any way. If he speaks a language other than English, those tests which use language should be given to him in the language he knows best. An interpreter must be provided for a deaf child where necessary. Braille, or other visual help, must be available for the visually handicapped.

6. PL 94-142 requires that every three years your special education child be given an additional thorough evaluation. This is to find out if he is in the appropriate education program. He may no longer need special education, or he may need services other than he is receiving at the present time.

7. At the conclusion of every evaluation, you should have the results explained to you satisfactorily. As we have said before, if you do not feel the school's evaluation is fair or accurate, you can ask for another evaluation by an outside evaluator.

Helping Parents Understand the IEP

When you talk with parents about their child's individualized education program, you'll want to incorporate these points:

1. The education plan for your child will be developed at a meeting to which you will be invited. PL 94-142 requires this. If you can't be at the meeting on the date set, ask the district to set it for a time when you can be there.

2. The education plan to be developed at the meeting is called an individualized education program (IEP). If your child is in special education, a school program has to be developed for him which meets his special needs—academic, emotional, and physical. You can have a copy of his IEP.

3. The people at the IEP meeting will include you, your child's teacher, and someone who is able to provide or supervise special education. In addition, your child can attend if this is appropriate. Also, you may want to bring someone (for example, another parent, who knows about IEPs). If this is the first time your child is considered for special education, the person(s) who tested him, or someone who can explain the testing, must be present.

4. Your child's individualized education program will be reviewed and revised at least once a year, and more often if you or the school feel it is necessary. You will be invited to these meetings.

5. It's a good idea to keep a file of all the things that have been done for your child. Bring this information to the IEP meeting. Use your right to examine your child's school records to be sure they are up-to-date and agree with your information.

6. After you have observed your child and have studied the results of his evaluation, be clear in your mind about what kind of school program you feel he is ready for. Listen to what others say at the IEP meeting and put in your own ideas. Back up what you say with your understanding of the evaluation and your observation of your child.

7. As your child's IEP is developed, be alert for such items as:

   a. The length of time he will spend in the regular classroom. Handicapped children should be educated in regular classrooms to the extent that it is beneficial to them.

   b. The goals stated for your child. The IEP goals shouldn't be general statements such as "Teach child basic math skills." They should be specific: "(The child) will be able to count from 1 to 100 on or before _____ (date)."

   c. Architectural barriers: Your child should not be excluded from a school program because of an architectural barrier. The district has the responsibility to remove the barriers, or deliver the program in a barrier-free location.

   d. The services your child is going to receive: Your child's special education and related services should be clearly described. For instance, if special transportation is necessary, the IEP should say when it will start and how long it will last. If speech therapy is offered, the IEP should say how often it will take place each week, how your child's progress will be measured, and so on.

   e. When you are satisfied with what has been accomplished at the IEP meeting, you are ready to give written permission for your child to receive the education and related services which are stated in his IEP. The name of the program will also be on the paper you sign. For example, program for the learning disabled, or the emotionally disturbed, or the mentally retarted, whatever the case may be. As you will see from your child's IEP, this designation doesn't mean he will be in a classroom, or even in a class or group, that has this kind of handicapping label. The designation does inform you of the handicapping condition your child has. This pinpointing of the disability is one of the results of the evaluation.

f. If you don't agree with the special education and related services the school district is offering, make an appointment to meet with the IEP team again to present what you believe will be a better program for your child. If further meetings result in non-agreement, you may ask for a due process hearing. While the hearing is in process, your child remains in his present school setting.

An administrator who presents the foregoing material will have gone a long way toward establishing a good, professional relationship with parents. In addition, here are some general suggestions which will strengthen that relationship.

Six Steps That Foster Good Relationships with Parents

1. Meetings with parents shouldn't be confrontations. They should be opportunities for honest sharing of information and careful planning for a child's future. Because parents have an understandable emotional reaction to their child's handicap, they may approach a meeting with special education people with tense, aggressive feelings in order to hide their true concerns. Don't try to make points with parents who are upset; rather, try to answer their questions as straightforwardly as possible without unnecessary elaboration. When parents understand you are really listening to them, and not trying to draw them away from their concerns

with speeches of your own, your relationship with them will strengthen.

2. Be frank in telling parents that you are interested in promoting better cooperation between them and the school personnel, where this is appropriate. Parents become rapid learners where their children are concerned. For example, an administrator of special education reports that after minimum instruction was given a group of parents about IEPs, a number of them came to their child's meeting with a written list of goals they wanted put into the child's education program. This involvement, which is unusual today, may be quite commonplace in a few years. Initiate good working relations with parents now.

3. Be sensitive to the knowledge and backgrounds of the parents. Respect all of them and realize some have made an effort to learn about education for handicapped children. Their knowledge and interest should be recognized. These parents make fine classroom volunteers and parent leaders.

4. Utilize what you learn from parents. They know more about their child than you. Seek to draw them out. Open up discussions so they are free to talk about their child and his problems. This leads to better student programming and parental satisfaction.

5. See that your district provides parents with learning opportunities which enable them to intelligently participate in their child's IEP. A parent who contributes nothing at the IEP meeting doesn't need criticism or pity; he needs training.

6. Parents need assistance in teaching appropriate skills and behaviors at home. If this service can be provided before school age, the school's efforts will be more productive.

These early intervention programs are costly; however, their worth has been proven. Also, when parents become actively engaged in their child's progress they become supporters of the school system, many times long after their child has completed his studies.

If priorities must be set, a rule of thumb might be to work with the young child and the young parent.

Summary

    Parents will become involved when they understand their role. The administrator of special education must inform parents of their legal rights. He must explain the part parents have in developing the IEP. He must listen to parents' input, and integrate this information into the child's school program. Parents have a strong voice in today's education.

Chapter Thirteen

Identifying the Administrator's Widening Area of Responsibility Under PL 94-142

An administrator makes things happen to others.

"A shot heard round the world," is how the renowned historian, Arnold Toynbee, characterized the American Revolution. In the world of American education, PL 94-142 can be compared to that shot. And like any revolution of consequence, its effects will be felt a hundred years or more. In our time, just a few years into PL 94-142, one of its most dramatic effects is the sudden widening of the special education administrator's area of responsibility. Today you face problems undreamed of a few years ago.

How to Attack the Goal of Full Education for the Handicapped, Ages 3-21

Knowledge of what your problems are in this regard is a step toward a good attack. A story will point out some barriers to be overcome. It concerns the preschool handicapped population, one of your extended parameters:

Not very long ago, an administrator of special education, wanting to help with the education of preschool children, read that the federal government was funding projects for this purpose. He wrote a fine project and obtained permission from district authorities to receive federal funds for it; and for three years his district had a model program going for very young children. Then came surprise time. The federal funding ended and his district was faced with the reality that district money would have to be the financial resource to keep the project going. The school board didn't feel the district could afford to take on this added expense, but by this time the program was so entrenched that it was impossible to discontinue it without causing criticism from some very vocal parents. "So," as the special administrator said, "the public wouldn't stand for us to discontinue the program, nor would the board give us money for its continuance; and there we were, 'holding the bag.'"

This isn't an unusual occurrence. A good use of your time regarding the education of young handicapped would be to endorse the efforts of those seeking to pass legislation to secure state support for the education of this population.

At the same time, you'll recall that a district is not required under PL 94-142 to provide for handicapped children aged 3-5 and 18-21 if state law expressly prohibits or does not authorize this expenditure, or if the provision is inconsistent with a court order. These "if's" are exceptions, of course. The intent of the law is education for the handicapped, 3-21 years.

Planning for Pre- and Post-School Age Children

If today's interest in the very young child foretells the future, it seems safe to say that in a few years the education of the preschool handicapped will be the legal responsibility of every school district in our country. Thus, special education administrators will want to begin planning for the attainment of the federal goal of education for handicapped children, 3 years and up. As soon as they see themselves able, districts will do well to accept federal support for their start-up programs in this area.

The education of the handicapped aged 18-21 is an easier task. These students are already in school; transportation and other related services are in operation. Their IEPs are written and the high school facility is already accommodating their special needs.

There's one important bit of advice, however. The administrator of special education will want to be careful about how these boys and girls are paced throughout their school years.

Some school systems have promoted the handicapped students right along with their peer group. They enter high school at about fourteen years of age, with the possibility of spending six or seven years there, as opposed to the normal four. And, as one special education teacher put it, "This creates a glut of students at the upper end of the high school program." She also remarked that, as she was the only resource room teacher in her high school, she has had some students for as long as seven years. Too long for one teacher. Thus, the numbers of handicapped students who choose to remain in school until their twenty-second birthday can become a problem, unless some forethought is paid to this eventuality along the way.

Since many of these students will have exhausted the academic benefits a regular high school can give them after four years, off-campus work-study placement should be written into their IEPs whenever they can profit from the experience.

Tips on Alternate Ways to Serve Handicapped Children

Besides what your special education offers, there are other resources for the education of handicapped children.

Many states provide educational facilities for children who are deaf, blind, deaf-blind, or have other severe handicaps such as profound retardation. (In some instances the services are initiated before the child reaches school age.) When children with the above handicaps are brought to your attention, your state operated schools should be investigated. Also, when faced with the problem of providing a service your special education program is not prepared to deliver, investigate the district's regular programs. For example, a special art class or a behavior modification program given for regular students may be just what the IEP designated for one of your district's handicapped pupils.

In summary, we can say that sources for meeting specific needs of some children include:

1. State operated schools.
2. Division of Vocational Rehabilitation (secondary students).
3. Department of Mental Health (state and local).

4. State Department of Special Education.
5. University based clinics.
6. Medical schools (handicapped children's division).
7. Children's hospitals.
8. Approved private facilities (special reading centers, group homes).
9. Private psychiatric clinics and residential treatment facilities.
10. Department of Youth Services (juvenile detention homes).
11. Department of Public Health (municipal and county).
12. Private schools (residential or day).

From these agencies you can contract for the following services:

Medical (diagnosis)   Inservice training
Psychological   Transportation
Social Work   Speech and hearing
Educational   Therapy
Job training and placement

You will probably consider contracting for the above services for the following reasons:

1. The service you must provide is of low incidence in your district.
2. The cost effectiveness of the contracted service is demonstrated.
3. Your district has need for additional trained personnel that aren't available at the time.

Key Factors in Contracting Services from Other Agencies

Precautions are taken when entering into contractual agreements. Perhaps the most important one is that all components of the agreement are in writing. The contract should include the following:

1. The legal identification of your district.
2. Specification of services your district is contracting for.
3. The duration of the contract.
4. The legal identification of the organization or individual who is to provide the service.

5. An evaluation component of the services which are to be provided.

6. Specification and designation of financial responsibilities.

7. Specification of any additional responsibilities (insurance, etc.).

8. Signatures of contractual parties.

Prior to finalizing an agreement, your district should clarify the following:

1. The eligibility, by age group, for students; especially for those 3-5 and 18-21 years.

2. The physical facilities where the contracted service will be delivered. Are they adequate? Are there architectural barriers?

3. Is the program management satisfactory?

4. How is the program supervised?

5. How are equipment and supplies to be provided?

6. Are there conflicts with school calendars?

7. Are substitute teachers to be provided?

8. What are the program referral procedures?

9. How are reports to be handled? By whom? In what form?

10. Who takes charge of attendance?

11. How is student discipline handled?

12. Is transportation included in the contract? What does it include?

13. What are the administrative costs and services?

14. What is the professional status of personnel involved?

15. Has a determination of each agency's financial responsibility been established?

With these questions answered satisfactorily, you should have no major problems with the contracting agency. The following lists some services which are free of charge:

1. Division of Vocational Rehabilitation:
    a. Vocational evaluation and training
    b. Work-study programs
    c. Vocational counseling

    d. Job placement and follow-up services

    e. Sheltered workshops and other subsidized situations

2. Department of Health:

    a. Diagnosis and evaluation

    b. Medical services pertaining to diagnosis and evaluation

    c. Physical and occupational therapy

    d. Speech and hearing services

    e. Vision screening

    f. Dental services

3. Department of Mental Health:

    a. Psychological examination and further referral as needed

    b. Psychological services

    c. Training and education of some developmentally disabled children

    d. Education services for severely and profoundly handicapped children in state schools

Key Points in Handling Procedural Safeguards

Because procedural safeguards include parental involvement, IEP development, confidentiality of information, and due process hearing, an administrator's reputation — and at times even his job — will depend to a great extent on how well he carries out this requirement. Procedural safeguards widen your area of responsibility more than any other aspect of PL 94-142.

A number of references have already been made regarding the procedural items; in this section we'll summarize all the information in one place, in order for you to see as a totality what comprises this part of the law. Tips on handling the procedures, which are not discussed elsewhere in this handbook, are also given in this section.

Our first suggestion is that procedural safeguards should be in writing. To be fully covered, you should not only *do* what is required, but also have in *writing* what is being done. Now let's examine the items themselves.

1. Handling Confidential Records

The person keeping files up-to-date and filling requests for records should be able to consult a written directive which reflects these considerations:

a. The child's records contain information on his identification, evaluation, and educational placement.

b. If other children are identified in child X's records, this information is blocked out before the parent of child X is given the record.

c. The request for a record is fulfilled without unnecessary delay (in no case more than 45 days), and before any meeting takes place involving the record.

d. Your district responds to reasonable requests for explanations and interpretations of records.

e. Copies of records are provided to a parent when failure to do so would deprive him of his right to inspect his child's records.

f. An authorized representative of the parent has the right to inspect the records.

g. A parent doesn't have authority to inspect records if your district has been legally advised that under state law governing such matters as guardianship, separation, and divorce the parent hasn't the right of inspection.

h. Authorized employes of your school district, or other participating agencies, do not need parental authorization in order to inspect records.

i. Your district keeps a record of persons obtaining access to records, except access by parents, authorized employes of your school district, and other participating agencies.

j. If the records are in more than one place, your district informs parents where the records are.

k. A parent who believes that records are inaccurate, misleading, or in violation of privacy and other rights may request your district to amend the information.

l. If your district decides to refuse to amend the records, you inform the parent of this and advise him of his right to a due process hearing in this regard.

2. The Independent Educational Evaluation

a. If a parent is dissatisfied with your district's evaluation and requests an independent evaluation, your district must pay for this unless your district initiates a hearing and the hearing officer decides the district's evaluation was satisfactory. The parent can go ahead with the independent evaluation, but at his expense.

b. Your district provides to parents, on request, information about where an independent evaluation may be obtained.

c. If a parent obtains an independent evaluation, the results are considered in any decision made with respect to the education of the child.

d. If a hearing officer requests an independent evaluation as part of a hearing, the cost of the evaluation is at school district expense.

e. Whenever an independent evaluation is undertaken, the criteria of the evaluation procedures are of the same quality which your district uses.

3. Prior Notice and Parental Consent

a. Written notice must be given to parents before your district either proposes, or refuses, to initiate or change the identification, evaluation, or educational placement of their child.

b. Written parental consent must be obtained before your district conducts a preplacement evaluation of a child and before initial placement in a special education program. Written consent is also necessary before a child's personally identifiable records are released.

c. If your state law requires parental consent before a child is evaluated or placed, your state's procedures govern how you override a parent's refusal to consent.

d. If there is no state requirement for consent, your district may use due process under PL 94-142. The procedures for this are described later in this section.

4. Content of the Prior Notice

The notice must include:

a. An explanation of procedural safeguards available to parents. (See Chapter 11, Figure 11-7.)

b. A description and explanation of the action proposed or refused by your district, any options your district considered and, if appropriate, the reasons why those options were rejected.

c. Any other factors relevant to a change in a child's education.

d. Language understandable to the general public, and then put in a form that communicates best with the parents. If parents speak in a foreign language, are blind, or deaf, the communication must make provision for these circumstances.

5. The Due Process Hearing

Parents, your school district, or any public educational agency may initiate a hearing on any matter pertaining to a child's special education and related services. Due process includes the following:

a. Any hearing must be conducted by the state educational agency, or a public agency (your school district) which is directly responsible for the education of the child.

b. No matter who initiates a hearing, your school district must inform parents of free or low-cost legal services and other appropriate services.

Comment: Many districts are using mediation instead of a due process hearing. Mediation resolves differences without the development of the hostile relationships so often associated with legal procedures. The mediations are conducted by members of SEAs, or LEAs not previously involved in the case. For an informal approach to mediation see "Try Mediation Instead of Litigation," in Chapter 14.

6. The Hearing Officer

Your SEA will probably be your resource. Regulations under PL 94-142 give the following meager directives:

a. A hearing may not be conducted by an employe of an agency involved in the education or care of the child, or by a person whose interests would conflict with objectivity.

b. Your district shall keep a list of hearing officers and their qualifications.

c. The selection of a hearing officer must be agreed on by both parties.

7. Hearing Rights

a. Any party to a hearing has the right to:

1. Be accompanied and advised by counsel and by individuals with special knowledge about handicapped children.

2. Present evidence and confront, cross-examine, and compel the attendance of witnesses.

3. Prohibit the introduction of any evidence at the hearing which has not been disclosed to that party at least five days before the hearing.

4. Obtain a verbatim record of the hearing.

5. Obtain written findings of facts and decisions relevant to the hearing. (Your district must transmit those findings and decisions, after deleting any personally identifiable information, to your State Advisory Panel on Special Education.)

b. A parent has the right to:

1. Have his child, who is the subject of the hearing, present at the hearing.

2. Open the hearing to the public.

8. Appealing a Hearing Decision

The decision made by the hearing officer is final unless one of the parties appeals. The appeal is subject to the following conditions:

a. If the hearing was conducted by a local district, either party may appeal to the SEA. If there is an appeal, the SEA must conduct an impartial review of the hearing. The review shall:

1. Examine the entire hearing record.

2. Insure that the procedures at the hearing were consistent with requirements of due process.

3. Seek additional evidence if necessary.

4. Afford the parties opportunity for oral and written argument at the discretion of the reviewing official.

5. Make an independent decision, on completion of the review.

6. Give a copy of written findings and the decision to the parties involved.

b. The decision made by the SEA reviewing official is final, unless one of the parties brings a civil action suit.

9. Timelines and Convenience of Hearings and Reviews

a. Within 45 days from the date of receipt of a request for a hearing, your district must conduct the hearing and mail a copy of the decision to each of the parties. The same tasks must be performed by your SEA, not later than 30 days after the receipt of a request for a "review of a hearing" is received. At the request of either party, these time periods may be extended.

b. Each hearing and each review must be conducted at a time and place reasonably convenient to the parents and child involved.

10. Child's Status During Proceedings

Unless your district and the parents agree otherwise, the child remains in his present educational placement during the hearing. With parental consent, a school aged child not in school must be placed in a school program while proceedings take place. This does not preclude your district from using normal procedures for dealing with children who are endangering themselves or others.

11. Confidentiality of Information

In addition to other references pertaining to the importance of confidentiality, we include these:

a. One person in your district assumes responsibility for the confidentiality of personally identifiable information.

b. Persons collecting or using personally identifiable information must receive instruction regarding confidentiality requirements under PL 94-142.

c. Your district must maintain for public inspection a current listing of the names and positions of employes who may have access to personally identifiable information.

d. Your district must inform a parent when the identifiable information regarding his child is no longer needed. This information must be destroyed if the parent so requests. (A record of a student's name, address, his grades, attendance record, classes attended, grade level completed, and year completed, may be maintained.)

e. Your district should remind parents that identifiable records may be needed in the future for social security benefits or other purposes.

f. Your SEA must have available for parents a summary of the policies and procedures your district must follow regarding storage, disclosure to third parties, retention, and destruction of personally identifiable information. This information must be made available to parents prior to the time the SEA and LEA undertake any major identification, location, or evaluation activity.

12. Children's Rights

Under the regulations of a law titled the "Family Educational Rights and Privacy Act," the rights of parents regarding education records are transferred to the student at age 18, where the transfer is appropriate.

The last four items on procedural safeguards have been discussed previously. Three of them are in Chapter 11: (1) Evaluation, (2) Placement, and (3) Review of the IEP. The fourth item, Least Restrictive Environment, is presented in Chapter 8.

Summary

The enlarged parameters of responsibility for an administrator of special education remain the most dramatic effect of PL 94-142. Chief among the administrator's new jobs is the task of carrying out programs in compliance with the many requirements under procedural safeguards. Another extension of duties is providing an appropriate education for children aged 3-5 and 18-21.

Chapter Fourteen

Guidelines for
Taking Legal Precautions

The concern about appearing stupid can prevent you from asking many important questions.

In the jungle of "do's" and "don't's" the administrator of special education finds himself in as he implements his program, none are as important as the guidelines that see him through without the threat of a law suit. We're not referring to the administrator, or district, that deliberately invites legal action in order to prove the legality of some activity. Rather, our purpose is to present safeguards for the administrator who doesn't want his district to be taken to court because of carelessness or ignorance of the law on his part, or on the part of others with whom he works. Let's look at some ways to help avoid this situation.

Trouble Spots in the Laws

Existing federal laws require that close attention be paid to these facts:

1. Architectural barriers: The accessibility and use of facilities by the handicapped in your district's schools.

2. Employment of district personnel: The questions you can and cannot ask potential employes; the handling of medical examinations for potential employes; and the implementation of affirmative action in hiring practices.

3. Civil rights of the handicapped as they pertain to education: Avoiding discrimination against children because of race, religion, culture, or ethnic background.

4. Public Law 94-142: The provision of an appropriate education for the handicapped; and safeguarding the rights of handicapped children and their parents.

Remember, handicapped children can be members of other protected populations also. Children who are mentally retarded or visually impaired can belong to a racial minority or be children of migrant parents. The point is, then, that your job is to see handicapped children receive an appropriate education which precludes any wrongful discrimination or practice under any circumstance, as regards their public education.

Watch Out for the Procedural Safeguards

The contents and implementation of the safeguards are given in Chapter 13. Here, we'll point out some precautionary measures. Let's start with this observation: If someone is asked which sections of PL 94-142 are the most important, the response is the services and procedural safeguards. If asked the reasons for this choice, the logical answer would be: (1) services include the IEP, a primary goal of the law; and (2) procedural safeguards deal with people's civil rights, a precious possession they'll go to law to defend.

To this we'll add the warning that a slip-up is likely to occur more often in procedural safeguards than in any other part of the law. Here's a case in point:

A family with a handicapped child of primary age moved in to a particular district. The parents didn't respond to the invitation to come in for a discussion of their child's education. However, they did consent to an evaluation by signing the written consent form and mailing it in to the administrator of special education. The school psychologist was notified and scheduled a time to administer a WISC. Then the special education administrator had second thoughts on the subject. He recalled that procedural safeguards state that where appropriate, tests should be in the child's native language. Was the district sure English was the home language? The family name indicated otherwise. The little child hardly spoke at all, and the only communication with the parents had been their signature on the permission form. The family had no phone; so the administrator took time to call at the home. He discovered that the parents spoke Spanish and had signed the permission form only after an older boy, who spoke and read a little English, had shown them where their signature was requested. After uncovering this information, an interpreter was employed and other necessary safeguards followed.

This incident shows how careful you have to be in protecting the civil rights of parents and children. The district could have gone ahead with the traditional evaluation procedures and developed an IEP that no one could fault — unless, of course, a monitor of the district's special education procedures, or a legal aide assigned to the family, or any other advocate, uncovered the slip-up. Then a law suit could easily have been brought against the district.

Remember Parents' Rights

We've already given the most important advice for this section: enclose a copy of parents' rights (see Chapter 11, Figure 11-7) with every notice sent to parents regarding their child's education. But there are other things to watch for as well.

Should a parent decide to have a hearing, the process requires careful adherence to legal procedures (see Chapter 13), and you can expect some expense for legal counsel. Some districts have gone the economical route and carried out the hearing without this counsel; but this often ends in an unfavorable situation for the district. A parent isn't going to enter into a due process hearing unless he means business, and should he lose his case it's only to be expected that a search for procedural errors will be made to help swing an appeal in his favor.

A district should realize that it is in a vulnerable position when it is party to a hearing. Appeals and law suits are not unusual outcomes. Your district should be sure of itself every step of the way, and the administrator of special education should be ready to aid the district when special education is involved in the legal action. Keep these facts in mind in regard to hearings:

1. There is little information given in the law regarding hearing officers.

2. Your state has statutes and rules pertaining to general due process hearings which should be investigated.

3. Your SEA should be contacted for assistance, including suggestions for hearing officers.

Try Mediation
Instead of Litigation

If thoughts about due process hearings weigh heavily on your shoulders, this paragraph should lighten the burden. It deals with mediation as a means of avoiding hearings. Here's how a meeting successfully avoided a law suit:

> Nineteen-year-old Joey is a Down's syndrome child in a high school special education program. His parents were not satisfied with his curriculum; he wasn't allowed into a photography class which they thought he would enjoy and would also be useful to him. They threatened legal action, so a meeting was called to try to resolve the problem. Attending were Joey, his parents, the school principal, the administrator of special education, the special education teacher, and a director of the state's Association for Retarded Citizens. To insure Joey's rights, the administrator of special education explained the purpose of the meeting to the boy.
>
> The meeting evolved around the potential dangers for Joey in the photography class — for example, the mixing of chemicals, the darkroom, and going around the campus taking pictures. The parents insisted Joey could handle these things. Finally, the district said it would hire an aide to assist the boy in this particular course. The parents agreed.

As your district's administrator of special education, you will note how the meeting was conducted and the personnel attending. Did you notice how careful the special education administrator was in explaining to Joey the purpose of the meeting? Joey is over eighteen and must be included in procedures regarding his education wherever appropriate.

The results of this meeting will cost the district money for Joey's aide. But public hearings are costly, too, and the school personnel decided they would rather spend funds on something that would help the boy and satisfy the parents, instead of spending them on due process.

Don't Act Hastily — But Act

To the above suggestion we add this consideration: Not to act hastily doesn't mean to go slowly; rather, it means that you shouldn't *decide* hastily. Take all the time you need to make a good decision, but use that time to work at arriving at a good solution to the problem — especially if you're into a problem involving legal repercussions. And in today's special education world there are very few problems that don't have legal overtones.

As soon as a problem presents itself, start to work on it. When possible, discuss the legal aspects with a school district attorney. Or call the special education division of your SEA and talk with their specialists. They will give you advice as well as sources for legal counsel. Review your state's statutes and rules and your district policies as they relate to the problem.

This reviewing of statutes and policies takes time, but after you do a thorough checking a few times, you'll begin to remember laws and rules, and the time you spend on them will be considerably shortened. But no matter how long it takes, our advice is to do it, and to start now. More than one educational leader has remarked that it practically takes a lawyer to administer today's special education. Well, you may not be a lawyer, but you can be conversant with laws and rules relevant to your field. Here's an example of an administrator who almost learned this lesson too late.

Once there was a fairly new administrator who thought that at least some of his problems would go away if he put them aside. He didn't like to dig in. One persistent thorn in his side was a mother who pestered him to arrange bus transportation for her child. The family lived five blocks from the school and the child, although handicapped, knew the route and could manage the walk. The administrator kept putting the mother off. He wasn't sure what action to take and figured the problem would disappear if he did nothing. But it didn't, and in time the thing had dragged on so long that he was embarrassed to ask his superior for advice, for fear he'd be asked when the mother first wanted the service and what he'd done about it thus far. After three months, when the parent was threatening to sue, he finally sought an answer and the situation was cleared up quickly. District policy stated that a primary child would either have to live more than eight blocks from school, or be unable to manage the route on his own, before being considered for transportation services.

The special education administrator was actually very good in his field, and at the time he told the mother about district transportation policy he had a long talk with her about her child. The mother was appreciative of the life-time goals the school had for

handicapped children, one of which was to make them as independent as possible. So the incident ended on a positive note.

How differently this story would have turned out if the special
education administrator had continued to let things slide, and the
impatient parent had demanded a hearing — and once demanded
wasn't going to be put off.

Be Careful About
What You Say and Write

Let us assume you have been given a problem to solve. You
have reviewed the laws and rules, sought appropriate advice, and
acted with deliberate speed. Now you're ready to give your answer.
How can you do this to the best advantage? We advise you again to
take all the time you need; this time to formulate your ideas into
clear, concise statements. Often an administrator understands the
statutes and regulations but he can't express his ideas either in writing or orally. Misunderstandings take place when he attempts to
explain something, and if his poor explanation involves a serious
matter, serious misunderstandings follow. Here's an example:

> An administrator of special education engaged a psychometrist
> to help out in the district's psychological testing program. The
> administrator thought he had told the examiner it was neces-
> sary to have written parental permission before psychological
> tests could be given. But the examiner hadn't understood it
> that way and the district wound up being sued by a parent for
> testing his child individually without first getting his written
> permission. That's a hard way to learn a lesson.

If you feel frustrated when you are consistently misinterpreted,
or when your directives aren't followed, perhaps the fault lies with
you. Start now to plan how you will state your next announcement;
how you will explain your next decision; and how you will defend
that decision orally and in writing. To explain an important point
about which you are informed without a plan of delivery might result in the same dissatisfaction that would occur if you weren't
informed. And that's unfortunate, because you are knowledgeable;
you've done your homework. So make it pay by carefully doing the
next step — planning how you'll share your information. We all
know that in a law suit it's almost always the district that gets sued.
But if the suit arises out of some misunderstanding in the special

education department, such as in the above incident with the school psychologist, the district is going to take a long look at the person in charge of special education.

Tips on Administering
Medication to Students

No doubt your district has a policy concerning medications being administered by personnel. Be sure the special education teachers are aware of this. For districts without a written policy, the following list suggests some specifications:

1. No teacher can be required to administer medication.
2. If a teacher does administer medication, she and the building principal should have, on file, information from the student's doctor which includes:
   a. The doctor's description of time and method of administration.
   b. The prescription and recommended dosage.
   c. Possible reactions to the medication.
   d. Parental signature for the teacher to administer medication.
3. The teacher should be alerted that she may be held negligent and personally liable to court action if a mistake is made by her in administering medication.
4. Prescription medicine may not be brought to school by a student for self-administration without his doctor's written approval. The approval should be filed in the principal's office.
5. In a school that employs a full-time registered nurse, medications should be locked in the nurse's office.
6. In schools that employ a less than full-time registered nurse, the medication should be locked in the principal's office.

Be Prepared to
Respond to Disruption

The best way to assure an effective response to disruption is through cooperative pre-planning. Most districts have policies, both written and unwritten, regarding disruptions. It's a good idea to review these policies and see if they adequately provide for all categories of handicapping conditions. Basically, they should include the following points:

1. The district's serious problems are identified, including those which are school-centered, community-centered, or a combination.
2. The local police are aware of serious problems and feel free to suggest ways to prevent and handle disruptions.
3. There are adequate resources within the school and community to implement solutions to problems as they arise, or to do away with them altogether.
4. There is a fair code of discipline and a Student Bill of Rights in practice in the schools.
5. Students, parents, and staff are involved in handling disruptive problems.
6. The staff is able to deal with handicapped students' problems without undue disturbance or antagonism.
7. Potential problem sites are identified and supervised. These include restrooms, gyms, cafeteria, boiler rooms, bus zones, and athletic fields.
8. There is a clearly defined chain-of-command for school personnel when a disruption occurs.
9. The staff is given operation instructions concerning adverse incidents. These include:
   a. How to assist injured students, including students with handicapping conditions.
   b. How disruptive students can be removed from the problem site.
   c. How to communicate quickly with parents.
   d. A list of emergency telephone numbers (police, fire, ambulance, etc.).

Liability and Teachers' Rights

"School boards and administrators who want to evaluate teacher performance ought to evaluate their own chances of getting sued first," states a national education service agency. This particular agency has developed an inservice on the legal issues in teacher evaluation. The course revolves around three teachers protesting their board's failure to renew their teaching contracts. At least one small district wishes their personnel had taken the course. It has the dubious distinction of being the first district in its state found guilty of firing a teacher without first giving her an opportunity for a hearing. The fine was something over $4,000, quite a budget bite for the tiny community.

To help your district avoid litigation when it is considering terminating a teacher, we'll summarize the points we made in Chapter 7 under "Hints on Terminating Employment."

1. Have documented data on hand to back up any charge you make.
2. Show the data to the teacher and discuss it with her.
3. Keep the data under lock and key.
4. Keep a calendar record of all meetings and other incidents that pertain to a teacher and the retention of her job.
5. Be sure your state's due process procedures are followed. The teacher's right to a hearing is one of the procedural safeguards.

Here Are Some Extra "Do's" So You Won't Be Sued

1. Annually review:
   a. How handicapped students' discipline is handled.
   b. Your accident/injury procedures, including students on work experience.
   c. Your student record-keeping procedures.
   d. Your transportation policy for field trips.
2. Develop written guidelines for substitute teachers who have handicapped children in their classes. Substitute teachers should know:
   a. Who the handicapped children are in the classroom.
   b. What to do in emergencies (fires, bomb threats, seizures, etc.).
3. Develop a written policy for treating playground injury.
4. If you have a corporal punishment policy, put it in writing and get proper approval.
5. Inform your superintendent, in writing, of situations and

equipment that might be dangerous for handicapped students.

6. Require written rules for all field trips off school property.

And here are some "Do's" for teachers to help both them, and you, avoid being involved in a legal suit.

1. Develop rules for the classroom, in writing, and make them consistent with board of education policy.
2. Contact parents of students causing behavior problems.
3. Document violations of room policy.
4. Never leave a classroom unsupervised.
5. Require adequate supervision on field trips. One adult to one student may be necessary at times.
6. Never dismiss a student to run a non-educational errand.

Summary

Procedural safeguards are a vital component of special education; they govern the way special education is carried out. Directives under procedural safeguards should be in written form. Written policies for each area of your program are one of your best safeguards against litigation. These areas include health services, field trips, fire prevention and safety, and employment practices.

Chapter Fifteen

Important Considerations for the Special Education Administrator

I was so busy cutting down the trees that I didn't take time to sharpen my axe.

Every step taken in special education is worth consideration. Previously, we've dealt with items important enough to be chapters in themselves. Here, we'll discuss activities that are of high priority but don't fall into any of the foregoing material.

How to Be Monitored Successfully

"What do you do when you're about to be monitored?" is a question aimed at the district administrator of special education. You could respond as St. Thomas of Aquinas did when asked what he would do if the end of the world was coming within the hour. "Why, I would just continue what I'm doing now, sit here and read philosophy," he answered. St. Thomas' composure is expected of a saint, but for lesser mortals, both the announcement of the world's end and the knowledge of a monitoring visit by our SEA will cause some flutterings to say the least.

But the prospect shouldn't be too disconcerting if you know the requirements and what part your district has in them. Under PL 94-142 the SEA must advise you of its monitoring procedures, which include:

1. Collection of special education data and reports from your district. They'll tell you the kind and scope of the needed data.

2. On-site visits to your district by the SEA monitoring team. A mutually convenient time will be arranged.

3. A comparison of your district's written individualized education programs with the programs actually going on. The review team will visit classrooms.

4. Timelines for evaluation. Your district should be monitored at least once every three years.

The following questions should be answered in the affirmative. They're similar to those your SEA will ask during the monitoring:

1. Does your district have a policy specifying the goals of its child-find program?

2. Can you show evidence of how your district locates and identifies handicapped children not in school?

3. Does your district have a public awareness program for finding these children?

4. Can you show evidence that your district has a plan for screening students for referral to special education?

   a. Does the plan include screening agents other than teachers? (Parents, physicians, other school personnel.)
   b. Does the screening take in all areas where children may have difficulties? (Gross and fine motor skills, speech, language, health, vision, hearing, and social and academic skills.)
   c. Do you have screening procedures for the various levels and ages? (Pre-school, elementary, secondary.)

5. Can you show evidence that your district's evaluation procedures include assessments in all fields?

Medical	Adaptive social behavior
Psychological	Educational
Communication	Other

6. Can you demonstrate what your district does with a referral within 30 days of the referral date?

7. Can you give evidence that professional activities are carried out by qualified personnel?

8. Can you show evidence that accommodations are made when the child or his parents communicate in other than English?

9. Can you show how your district informs parents about the results of the evaluation?

10. Can you randomly select a student and show that his placement in special education is consistent with your state's eligibility criteria for the handicapping category you've placed him in? (Eligibility for special education is developed by SEAs, the one exception being the learning disabled criteria, which have been developed under PL 94-142. Chapter 5 presents the criteria for this group.)

11. Can you show evidence that no single type of test is used to determine a child's need for special education? (An exception might be speech.)

12. Can you present evidence that your district sends "prior notice" to parents? Does the notice include the parents' rights under PL 94-142?

13. Can you show evidence that your district has written parental permission, before it:
    a. Evaluates a child?
    b. Initially places him in special education?
    c. Releases personally identifiable information about him?

14. Can you present evidence that evaluations are racially and culturally non-discriminatory?

15. Can you show evidence that IEPs:
    a. Are developed by an appropriate team?
    b. Include a statement of annual goals and short term objectives, and criteria for determining their attainment?

16. Can you show evidence that a thorough evaluation is conducted for each child at least every three years?

Parents and Monitoring

The above questions are not all-inclusive. For example, some SEAs include parent interviews in their monitoring. Here are questions that might be asked of a parent:

1. Did you sign forms giving written permission for evaluation of your child?

2. Is your child integrated with nonhandicapped students in programs such as art, music, PE, or academics?

3. How do you feel about the education program being provided for your child?

4. Have you seen the individualized education goals specifically drawn up for your child?

5. Do you receive regular reports from the school about your child's progress?

6. Does the school re-evaluate your child each year? Are you invited to help with this?

7. Do you know if you can get an independent evaluation of your child outside the school system?

8. If you have a question about your child, who would answer it for you?

9. Are you satisfied with the transportation arrangements for your child?

Hints on the Mechanics of Monitoring

A typical monitoring by an SEA goes like this:

1. A number of weeks prior to the on-site review, the district superintendent and the administrator of special education are consulted as to the date of the review and the procedures to be followed.

2. On the agreed date, the SEA team conducts an entrance interview with school district personnel to present an overview of the SEA's objectives and procedures for the monitoring.

3. On-site monitoring takes place.

4. Upon completion of the on-site tasks, the review team conducts an exit interview with district personnel; this time to provide general information regarding the review and to receive any additional information.

5. Approximately two weeks after the monitoring, a report is made in writing to the district superintendent. It presents findings related to compliance or noncompliance within each requirement under PL 94-142. Recommendations for

program improvements are presented. Commendations are made where appropriate.

6. Should a district disagree with the findings, a letter is sent to the SEA specifying reasons for disagreement. Subsequent contacts with the district are made by the SEA until both parties are satisfied that a complete and fair monitoring has been accomplished. The district is then given a specified time in which to correct noncompliance factors, should some exist.

Remember, noncompliance doesn't necessarily mean willful noncompliance. The primary purpose for monitoring is to improve your district's services, where necessary, by bringing them up to the standards set by PL 94-142.

Your district may be asked to make these preparations for the on-site review:

1. Have available all written documentation of district policies and procedures related to special education.
2. Have appropriate class lists available for the visitation team.
3. Inform school staff that an on-site program review team will be visiting your district.
4. Provide the team with map of district to aid visitors in locating schools.
5. Have space available at the district office and selected schools for review of building information by review team.

Tips on Making Facilities Safe for Children

Let's begin this section with the following illustration:

Once a teacher of elementary educable mentally retarded students asked her supervisor to evaluate an experience she had with her class, from the viewpoint of safety precaution. She was returning from recess with her group when there was a delay because a girl discovered she had lost her ring. The class returned to the playground to help look for it, with the exception of one boy who asked to go on into the building as he wanted to use the restroom. When the class returned to the building some ten minutes later, it was sheer luck that the teacher happened to be the one who pushed against the classroom door first. The boy who returned earlier had removed the hinge pins from the door's hardware and then had somehow set the door back up on the empty hinge holes so that no one could see there was anything amiss. The teacher felt the door give way at her touch and was quick and strong enough to prop it up. If a child has pushed on the solid wooden door, no doubt it would have fallen, and possibly a serious injury would have resulted.

The teacher's question had to do with whether a door with removable hinge pins was safe. The principal of the building, the supervisor of special education, and the teacher discussed the situation, and it was decided that, although admittedly the pins were removable and therefore not perfectly safe, safety codes can go just so far, and after that it is up to the teacher to be on the lookout for potential dangers. The district safety officer agreed. He said that dangers occur in so many situations that it is impossible to cover them all in a list of regulations. "Be alert to the possibility of injurious situations, keep a careful watch on the children, and don't let immature children be without adult supervision any more than you can possibly help," was the final advice of the safety officer.

The words, "Be alert of the possibility of injurious situations," ring a bell. The special education administrator will want to look for the following adaptations in facilities used by handicapped students:

1. Adjustable seating
2. Wide doorways
3. Nonskid floors
4. Ramps or elevators
5. Hand rails
6. Rounded corners
7. Doors with panic bars
8. Protected coat hooks
9. Hand bars by chalkboards, drinking fountains, and in toilet stalls

When selecting a building for a special education program, or when mainstreaming handicapped children into regular classrooms, the special education administrator should consider these standards:

1. The facility is approved by health, fire, and safety officials.
2. Food service is available and accessible to the handicapped.
3. Outdoor play areas are accessible and free from traffic hazards.
4. The facility has adequate and accessible toilet facilities.
5. The classrooms are comparable in size and condition to regular classrooms.

6. The classrooms have:
   a. Adequate ventilation and heating.
   b. Sufficient, safe storage space.
   c. Accessible and sufficient work space.
   d. Usable and sufficient furnishings.
   e. Adequate, glare-proof lighting.
   f. Accessible electrical outlets.
   g. Sufficient soundproofing where necessary.

Both regular and special teachers must be made aware that special precautions have to be taken with some handicapped students. A school's general safety plan is the responsibility of the building administrator; the modifications made for special education students are the responsibility of the special education administrator. You may want to inservice those who teach the handicapped on adaptive safety procedures. In Chapter 10 under "Special Classroom Requirements for the Handicapped," we mentioned instruction in emergency procedures as a necessity. Here, we present some guidelines for that instruction. For teachers who have in their classes:

1. Deaf and hard-of-hearing:
   a. Emergency/safety procedures are required study.
   b. Students demonstrate they understand the emergency/safety procedures.
   c. Each classroom teacher provides written fire-exit directions for the students.
   d. Students demonstrate that they understand the fire-exit route.
   e. A buddy system is used where appropriate. (A deaf student may need help when an emergency arises.)
   f. If the alarm system is solely a sounding alarm, some additions are made to alert a deaf student to an emergency. (A deaf student may be in a lavatory, or his buddy may be absent at the time.)
   g. The service of a teacher of the deaf is used, where necessary, to teach safety procedures.

2. Visually impaired:
   a. Emergency/safety procedures are read to, and discussed with, these students.
   b. Students demonstrate that they understand the procedures.

    c. Each classroom teacher provides oral fire-exit directions.

    d. Students demonstrate that they understand fire-exit route.

    e. A buddy system is used where appropriate.

    f. The service of a teacher of the blind is used, where necessary, to teach safety procedures.

3. Mentally retarded, learning disabled, emotionally disturbed:

    a. Emergency safety procedures are taught in ways understood by the students.

    b. Students demonstrate that they understand what to do in an emergency.

    c. Each classroom teacher provides oral or written fire-exit directions.

    d. Students demonstrate that they understand the fire-exit route.

    e. The buddy system is used.

    f. The service of a special education teacher is used, where necessary, to teach emergency/safety procedures.

4. Orthopedically impaired and other health impaired:

    a. Students understand emergency/safety procedures.

    b. Needed special equipment (wheel chairs, crutches, etc.) are always present in the room and easily available.

    c. The buddy system is used where appropriate.

    d. There are no architectural barriers which hinder or block an orthopedically impaired student from exiting from a building. (The exit time should be tested; it shouldn't be unreasonably longer than the exit time for normal students.)

Key Factors for Running a Better Transportation Program

You are a little handicapped child about nine years old. You board a bus every morning for the long ride to school. It takes at least forty minutes. The bus isn't like daddy's car; its seats are hard and you bounce around until your bones hurt. The windows are too high for you to see out of so you just sit there, restless and miserable. Around and around goes the bus on its daily route. Your breakfast feels funny; it's in your throat instead of your stomach. Sometimes you start crying for no reason that you can explain. Your teacher is concerned when you come into her classroom tearful and out of sorts. When you get home in the afternoon you're pale and exhausted. Your mommy worries about you.

This unfortunate situation is true in more cases than districts care to admit. And the sad part is that in many cases nothing can be done about it, short of the parents' moving nearer to the school.

Transportation is a vital component in the education of handicapped children. It becomes part of a student's IEP when school attendance necessitates special travel arrangements. Your district can use some of the federal funds you are entitled to under PL 94-142 for transportation. In some cases state reimbursement helps to a certain extent. Yet the real burden, both for expense and arrangements, rests within the district. Here are some helpful hints:

The person in charge of transporting the handicapped should work hand in hand with regular transportation personnel. Some administrators of special education make the mistake of arranging transportation that is already provided by the regular service. So a check on your district's services and routes is the first order of business.

If, after investigation, you find that your standard school bus service can't accommodate all the handicapped, you have other methods to opt for:

1. Public carriers other than regular school buses, such as specially designed mini-buses and vans: These vehicles are sometimes the property of school districts. If not, you probably can contract for them with a public transportation company or private agency.

2. Hiring Services: Some districts don't enter into contracts with transportation companies, preferring to hire the services on a monthly basis. This is a good idea if you're not sure of the company's reliability, whether it can give you all the service you need, or whether you'll need the service for a full contractual year.

3. Renting specially equipped vehicles: In this case, the school district hires the bus drivers and rents the specially designed cars or buses.

4. Sharing with another district the expense of owning or renting special vehicles: You might do this through your Intermediate Education Unit.

5. Taxi service: For short term, intermittent transportation, many districts use this service. Long term use of taxis is often made to transport the deaf, the blind, and other children whose handicap doesn't require special equipment or handling.

6. Private vehicles: This kind of transportation is sometimes done by parents. A district can't require a parent to do this; it can request it, however. The parent should be paid the rate per mile given state employees who drive their cars on official business.

Of major importance to the safe transportation of children is the skill and attitude of the driver. He should receive training to:

1. Be familiar with the special needs of handicapped children he's transporting.

2. Be aware of potential problems such as seizures and motion sickness.

3. Communicate emergency directions to children who can't hear, can't see, or can't communicate orally.

4. Handle specialized equipment.

5. Take unforeseen emergency action when necessary.

How to Serve Private School Children Under PL 94-142

There are two distinct ways your district may be involved in serving children in private schools.

First: Children in private schools who are placed there by their parents and are handicapped, or suspected of being handicapped, may be referred to the public school's special education program. They must be given all the services the public school children receive, including evaluation and offer of placement. They are protected by the same procedural safeguards. However, they must receive these services, including the implementation of their special education program, in the public school facility. Time schedules will have to be arranged for this to take place. Remember, your district doesn't pay tuition for children in private schools unless the district assigns them to the school. Remember, also, that it is your district's obligation to inform private schools in your area about the services you provide under PL 94-142.

Second: Children in public schools whose individualized education program necessitates their being served in private schools or other non-public school institutions will have their expenses, including tuition, paid by the public school district which assigns them. The district does not pay for medical treatment at the assigned institution, however.

When your district assigns a public school child to a non-public school agency, the responsibility for the child's education rests with your district. It is the public school's obligation to see that the child has an appropriate individualized education program, that procedural safeguards are observed, and that related services, such as satisfactory transportation and physical therapy, if needed, are provided.

Tips on Earning a Reputation for Being Resourceful

A resourceful person knows where to go for information, how to act in emergencies, and how to transfer skills employed in one area to another. He "makes do" with what's on hand while improving the general situation. The resourceful administrator of special education:

1. Has developed a good memory, or devices to aid a poor one. He hasn't time to write down everything he wants to act on as he goes about his duties, but when he has a minute he is meticulous in recalling and noting down things he said he would tend to.

2. Recognizes emergencies as part of his job.

3. Evaluates accidents as they occur. If they take on a pattern, he sets up an investigation as to causes and remediation.

4. Has developed a sharp eye for published materials that aid his programs. He knows he has it made when he hears a teacher respond to a colleague seeking a certain publication: "Go see Mr. Spec. Ed., he's got a system of educational information like I've never seen before."

Summary

To be monitored successfully, your district must demonstrate in writing and in action that it implements PL 94-142 as required. Safety of handicapped students, both in the building and when being transported, is an important consideration for the administrator of special education. As he succeeds at these, and all the tasks outlined in this handbook, he earns the reputation for being resourceful.

Appendix A

Analysis of Public Law 94-142
The Education for All Handicapped Children
Act of 1975

The purpose of this analysis is to provide the special education administrator with a summary of the actual law, divorced from its rules and regulations. The rules and regulations may change, but the law itself, as presented here, will probably remain intact for a number of years. We will start the analysis with Section 3 of the law, which pertains to findings and purpose.

I. Statement of Findings and Purpose

Prior to the enactment of PL 94-142, the Congress found that:

1. There are more than 8 million handicapped children in the United States today.

2. The special education needs of such children are not being met.

3. More than half of the handicapped children in the United States do not receive appropriate educational services.

4. One million of the handicapped children in the United States are excluded entirely from the public school system.

5. There are many handicapped children throughout the United States whose handicaps prevent them from having a successful educational experience because the handicaps are undetected.

6. Because of the lack of adequate services within the public school system, families are often forced to find services in private agencies.

219

7. Current state and local financial resources are inadequate to meet the special educational needs of handicapped children.

Purpose

It is the purpose of this Act to assure that all handicapped children have available to them a free appropriate public education which emphasizes special education and related services designed to meet their unique needs; to assure that children and parents' rights are protected; to assist states and localities; and to assure effectiveness of efforts to educate handicapped children.

II. Definitions	Implications for Local School Districts
1. Special Education: Free, specially designed instruction to meet a handicapped child's unique needs. It includes instruction in the classroom, home, hospitals, institutions, and in physical education.	Additional preservice and inservice training must be provided for personnel involved in special education. Careful diagnosis of handicapped children is a necessity. All children are to be provided for, regardless of handicap.
2. Related Services: Transportation and supportive services. These include speech, audiology, psychological, physical and occupational therapy, recreation, counseling, and medical (for diagnostic purposes).	Federal dollars can be used for related services when needed to enhance or provide specially designed instruction. Speech services can be considered either special education or a related service.
3. Free appropriate public education: Special education and related services which are at public expense, meet SEA standards, and are provided in conformity with the individualized education program (IEP) required herein.	Requires additional services and personnel, and additional personnel training.
4. Individualized Education Program (IEP): A written statement developed by LEA representative, teacher, parents, and child where appropriate. The contents include:	Requires development of administrative procedures to carry out requirements, and additional personnel training.
• Child's present level of educational performance.	Assignment of IEP teams.

- Annual goals and short term objectives.
- Specific educational services to be provided.
- Extent to which child will be able to participate in regular education programs.
- The projected date for initiation and anticipated duration of such services.
- Schedules for determining, at least annually, whether instructional objectives are being achieved.

5. Excess Costs: Costs in excess of annual average pupil expenditure in the district during preceding school year, after deducting amounts received under this part, or under Title I or Title VII (ESEA).

6. Native Language: Lanugage normally used by child or child's parents.

7. Intermediate Education Unit: SEA supervised agency which provides free public special education and related services on a regional basis.

III. Entitlements and Allocations

1. The maximum amount of the grant to which a state is entitled for a fiscal year equals the number of handicapped children served, age 3-21, multiplied by:

— 5% NAPPE (FY 1978) — $387 million

— 10% NAPPE (FY 1979) — $775 million

Parent involvement.

Inservice courses for regular teachers in reference to the teaching of handicapped children is needed. Procedural safeguards must be followed in undertaking the IEP tasks.

Excess cost will vary from district to district within a state.

Interpreters may be required.

IEU is similar to LEA in that it provides special education and related services to handicapped children. However, the LEA has the legal responsibility of providing an appropriate education for the children under its jurisdiction.

Implications for Local School Districts

Funding to LEA's increases annually by formula, until FY 1982. After 1982 the 40% figure remains firm. Actual dollar amounts will depend on (1) specifics in federal budget, and (2) the actual NAPPE for any current year. There is a limitation on the number of children a state may count for funding purposes. It is 12% of the number of all children

— 20% NAPPE (FY 1980) —
$1.2 billion

— 30% NAPPE (FY 1981) —
$2.32 billion

— 40% NAPPE (FY 1982) —
$3.16 billion

- Funds flow through your SEA. FY 1978 = 50% to SEA and 50% to LEA.
- FY 1979 and thereafter = 25% to SEA and 75% to LEA.
- In addition, 5% of total state allocation or $200,000, whichever is greater, is set aside for state administration of PL 94-142.
- The funds distributed by SEAs to LEAs are based on the local educational agency submitting an acceptable application to the state educational agency.

All local funds flow through the SEA from federal source.

Your LEA must prepare an appropriate application in order to receive funding. The SEA will assist your district with its application.

2. Federal dollars spent by the SEA for district and related services must be matched by state funds on a program by program basis.

No SEA may spend more Part B funds on support and direct services than its state spends on these services. A waiver of this requirement may be granted under certain conditions.

3. Federal funds spent by LEAs under PL 94-142 shall be used to supplement, and in no case to supplant, state and local funds.

4. No funds shall be distributed to an LEA if:

- The LEA is entitled to less than $7,500 for a fiscal year under the formula.
- The LEA has not submitted an acceptable application to its SEA for the funds.

5. Each LEA is entitled to an amount which bears the same ratio to the total amount available to all the LEAs in any state.

aged 5-17 in the state. The limitation applies to all states, regardless of age ranges served.

LEAs may form a consortium to generate the basic $7,500 needed.

SEA has responsibility for LEA PL 94-142 compliance in regard to the LEA application.

Example: A state's total of all LEA's shares is $300,000 for 20,000 children. District X has 3000 eligible children.

$$\frac{3000}{20,000} = 15\%;$$

15% of $300,000 = $45,000,
which is District X's share.

6. When no funds are distributed to a state where handicapped children reside, the SEA shall be responsible for seeing that special education is provided. Matching funds are not a requirement in this case.

The state educational agency must implement a special program where necessary.

7. 1% of the aggregate amounts available to all states is available to Guam, American Samoa, the Virgin Islands, and the Trust Territory of the Pacific Islands.

1% of the aggregate amounts available to all states is available for the education of handicapped children on Indian reservations.

8. If the sums appropriated for any fiscal year for making payments to states under PL 94-142 are not sufficient to pay in full the total amounts which all states are entitled to receive under the law for such fiscal year, the maximum amounts which all states are entitled to receive shall be ratably reduced. In case additional funds become available for making such payments for any fiscal year during which the preceding sentence is applicable, such reduced amounts shall be increased on the same basis as they were reduced.

Your LEA appropriation may ratably vary from the amount your district has arrived at by using the above formula.

IV. Eligibility

In order to quality for funding, a state must fulfill these conditions:

1. Have a policy which assures all handicapped children a free appropriate public education.

Implications for Local School Districts

Your SEA and LEA policies may have to be redirected.

2. The SEA must develop a plan, to be amended annually, which meets the criteria set up in PL 94-142, and it must submit the plan to the Commissioner of Education on an annual basis. The plan must include assurances that:

LEAs will be called on to implement their part of the plan.

- There is a goal of providing full educational opportunity to all handicapped children.

Additional training of personnel is needed.

- A detailed timetable is set for accomplishing such a goal.
- There is a description of the kind and number of facilities, personnel, and services necessary to meet such a goal.

Additional facilities and services may be needed.

- By September 1, 1978 a free appropriate public education will be available for all handicapped children between the ages of 3 and 18.

A waiver is possible regarding the education of children 3-5 and 18-21 years.

- By September 1, 1980 all handicapped children between the ages 3 and 21 will have this education available to them. This part of the requirement does not apply to the children aged 3-5 and 18-21, if it is inconsistent with state law or practice, or court order.

Special education programs are required if public education is provided for normal or handicapped children in the age groups 3-5 and 18-21.

- All children in need of special education are identified, located, and evaluated.

Child find and evaluation involves LEAs to a great extent.

- The confidentiality of personally identifiable information is assured.

LEAs must conform to procedural safeguards.

- The annual amended state plan (SEA's plan) must be available to the public 30 days prior to submission to U.S. Commissioner of Education.

LEAs will have their state's plan available to them for review and comment.

3. The following priorities must be set for service to handicapped children.

- First Priority: Handicapped children who are not receiving any education at all.
- Second Priority: Children with the most severe handicaps, within each disability area, who are receiving an inadequate education.

4. There must be assurance that each LEA will maintain, review, and revise as needed, but not less than once each year, an individualized education program (IEP) for each handicapped child.

Child find procedures must be developed.

Upgrading of services to handicapped children may involve more trained personnel. Programs must be evaluated to see which ones need upgrading.

LEAs must have a written individualized educational program for each handicapped child, which will be reviewed at least once a year. SEAs are required to evaluate your district's IEPs in accordance with criteria established under PL 94-142.

5. There must be assurance of procedures for procedural safeguards as required under PL 94-142. They will include:

- Procedures to assure that handicapped children will be educated with non-handicapped children to the maximum extent appropriate.
- Procedures to assure that testing and evaluation materials will be selected and administered so as not to be racially or culturally discriminatory.
- No single procedure shall be the sole criterion for determining an appropriate educational program for a child.

Training of regular teachers in instruction of handicapped children is needed.

Non-discriminatory evaluation a necessity. Culturally biased tests are not valid.

Multi-assessment teams are mandatory.

6. An assurance that all educational programs for handicapped children, including programs administered by any other state or

All educational programs for the handicapped, even those outside the state educational agency's authority, must meet SEA standards.

local agency, will be under the general supervision of the SEA and shall meet SEA standards.

7. An assurance that:

- Procedures are established for consultation with individuals involved in, or concerned with, the education of handicapped children.

  LEAs must have procedures for consulting with handicapped persons and their advocates regarding special education. An advisory board may be formed.

- There are public hearings regarding the development and implementation of special education, adequate notice of such hearings, and an opportunity for comment made available to the general public.

  LEAs will use the media to inform the public.

V. State Plan

Implications for Local School Districts

Each state (SEA) plan shall:

1. Set forth procedures that assure that funds paid to the state will be expended in accordance with the law.

Knowledge of entitlement formula and how the funds shall be spent is necessary. Examples: Division of funds between SEA and LEA; and formula for each district's share.

2. Provide that funds will be spent in a manner consistent with providing free appropriate public education for all handicapped children.

3. Set forth a description of procedures for:

- The development and implementation of a comprehensive system of personnel development.

  Inservice training at the LEA level is required.

- The adoption of promising educational practices and materials.

  The LEA should adopt promising practices developed through sound research.

4. Set forth procedures for the placement of handicapped children

Private schools must meet SEA and LEA standards. Qualified private in private schools by public school authorities, as a means of carrying out the children's IEPs. The education will be at no cost to parents.

5. Set forth procedures for the recovery of funds used for erroneously classified children.

6. Provide assurance that a qualified public agency will administer funds.

7. Provide for the necessary reports to be made to the Commissioner, and for the keeping of records of the reports.

8. Provide for an LEA to have reasonable notice, and opportunity for a hearing, before taking final action regarding the LEA's application for funds under PL 94-142.

9. Provide assurance that federal funds will not be co-mingled with state funds, and that the funds will not be used to supplant state and local funds — *except where the state provides evidence that all handicapped children have available to them a free appropriate public education,* in which case the Commissioner may waive the requirement of this clause.

10. Provide satisfactory assurance that proper disbursement is made of all funds.

11. Provide for an advisory board which includes handicapped individuals, teachers, and parents or guardians of handicapped children.

Duties of Advisory Board:

    a. Advise state on unmet needs in special education.

    b. Comment publicly on rules and regulations.

schools may participate in the education of handicapped children when the public school cannot perform the needed service.

SEAs will set procedures for recovery of misspent funds.

LEAs have time and opportunity to defend their application for funds under PL 94-142.

LEAs will be monitored by SEAs in relation to complying with this requirement.

Requires uniform procedures for monitoring of fund expenditures by the SEA.

The advisory board is the responsibility of the SEA.

LEAs will be concerned about the membership of the adivsory board.

   c. Assist SEA in developing and
        reporting on data.

12. Provide assurances that the
SEA will provide direct services
when necessary.

This provision takes place when
LEAs do not carry out needed
special education services and the
SEA must step in to do the job.

The SEA will be given reasonable notice and opportunity for a
hearing before the Commissioner
takes final action on a state plan.

VI. LEA Application

**Implications for Local School
Districts**

An LEA desiring funds must submit
an application to its SEA. The application shall:

1. Provide assurances that payments received will pay only for the
excess costs attributable to programs
which provide for:

Requires LEA applications for flow-
through money to contain all of the
assurances included in the state
plan, such as procedures for due
process, confidentiality, non-
discriminatory testing, full services
goal, and personnel training.

- Identification, location, and
  evaluation of handicapped
  children.
- Policies and procedures for
  assurance of confidentiality.
- Full educational opportunity
  for all handicapped children.
  This includes:

   a. A comprehensive system
   of personnel development
   established by the SEA.

Your district must participate with
the SEA in implementing a system
for personnel development.

   b. The setting of priorities
   for handicapped children not
   receiving any education, and
   for the most severely handicapped children within each
   disability, who are receiving
   an inadequate education.

Your LEA application must meet the
goals of the SEA as set forth in the
SEA's state plan.

   c. Parent participation.

   d. Special education and support services to enable handi-

Children must be placed in the least
restrictive environment. Special

capped children to participate in special education, and in regular education programs to the maximum extent practicable.

services in regular classrooms are necessary. Inservice training for regular teachers is needed.

2. Establish a full service time-table for providing full educational opportunity to all handicapped children.

Possible redirection of LEA policy.

3. Describe kind and number of facilities, personnel, and services necessary for full service.

Additional services and personnel may be needed.

4. Provide assurance that:

- Control of funds is in a public agency.
- Federal funds expended by LEAs will:
  a. Be for excess costs.
  b. Supplement, not supplant, existing fund expenditures.

LEAs will be monitored by the SEA regarding excess cost.

Federal dollars must be used to improve and embellish current programs, and to implement new programs. LEA expenditures for one year cannot be lower than the previous year.

5. Provide assurance that programs using federal funds are at least comparable to those programs not using federal funds.

Programs not receiving federal dollars must be as good in quality as similar programs that are receiving federal dollars.

6. Furnish information to the SEA relevant to the educational achievement of handicapped children. The LEA must keep records and provide access to records to the SEA.

LEA records may be examined by SEA.

7. Provide assurance that the application is available to the general public.

Your LEA application should be made public before submission to the SEA.

8. Provide assurance that individualized education programs (IEPs) will be established for each handicapped child and will be reviewed at least once annually.

Training teachers in development and implementation of programs is needed. Appointment of IEP teams is needed. Careful evaluation of handicapped children is needed. Increased administrative duties are apparent.

9. Provide assurance that local policies and programs will be established consistent with state plan as required in the law.

SEA assistance may be required to insure that LEA applications are consistent with SEA's state plan.

10. Provide assurance that procedural safeguards are established and maintained.

Examples: Confidentiality, due process, parent participation, prior notice, and parental consent.

11. The SEA must approve the LEA application. However, no LEA application may be approved until the federal government approves the SEA's state plan.

Federal approval of SEA plan required before SEA can approve any LEA application.

12. Whenever an SEA finds that a local education agency has failed to comply with requirements set forth in its application, after appropriate notice has been given, the state has the authority to cut off funds until compliance is met.

SEA has the authority to withhold LEA funds for reasons of non-compliance.

13. Whenever an LEA receives notice regarding cut off of funds, it shall take measures to call the matter to public attention.

SEA is the authority on LEA compliance. If funds are cut off, your LEA must make this known to the general public.

14. LEAs may form consortia in order to generate the minimum amount of money ($7,500) granted under PL 94-142. Also, an SEA may require LEAs that cannot establish a program of sufficient size and scope, or cannot generate the $7,500 minimum required to receive federal assistance, to form a consortium.

Some LEAs may be working together in order to receive funds under PL 94-142. The SEA will direct these efforts.

15. Consolidated application payments will be equal to the sum generated by each LEA involved in such a consolidation (consortium).

16. The SEA must write rules and regulations concerning the joint responsibilities of LEAs submitting consolidated applications.

LEAs must conform to SEA rules and regulations regarding consolidated applications (consortia).

VII. Direct Services by an SEA

1. An SEA will provide direct services if the SEA finds that:

- An LEA cannot meet requirements.
- An LEA is unwilling or unable to consolidate.
- An LEA has children that can best be served by a state facility.

2. An SEA must use the money that would have been available to LEAs, in order to provide the direct services to handicapped children which their LEAs are not providing for them.

Implications for Local School Districts

An SEA has the responsibility to determine when the state educational agency should provide direct services. State facility must be in compliance with PL 94-142.

No match requirement if an SEA establishes necessary programs that an LEA does not establish.

VIII. Funding Items

If a particular LEA is providing full service for all its handicapped students, an SEA may reallocate this LEA's dollars to other LEAs not providing adequate service. Federal funds cannot be used to reduce state and local expenditures.

Implications for Local School Districts

SEA determines where to distribute excess dollars.

IX. Procedural Safeguards

SEA and LEA must guarantee procedural safeguards. They include:

1. Opportunity for parents to examine records of identification, evaluation, and placement; and to obtain an independent educational evaluation of their child.

2. Protecting the rights of the child when parents are unknown, unavailable, or the child is a ward of the state. Includes appointment of a surrogate parent.

Implications for Local School Districts

Responsibility is placed on the SEA for assuring compliance with procedural safeguard requirements, and monitoring and auditing programs. LEA must comply with SEA monitoring procedures.

Requires training of surrogate parent. Surrogate parent shall not be an employe of SEA, LEA, or IEU involved in the education or care of the child.

3. Providing written prior notice to parents regarding change, or refusal to change, the identification, evaluation, and educational placement of a child, or the provision of a free appropriate public education.

In addition, written parental permission is required before an LEA can individually evaluate a child, or place the child in special education.

4. Giving parents the prior notice in their native language.

Money may have to be expended for interpreter or communication specialist.

5. Opportunity for parents to present complaints relating to identification, evaluation or placement of child in a program, or the provision of a free appropriate public education.

Parents must be made aware of this right.

6. Opportunity for parents to have an impartial due process hearing, conducted by SEA or by LEA as determined by state law or SEA. No employe of an agency concerned with education or care of the child shall conduct the hearing.

Training of hearing officers is needed. Also, the development of procedure for a hearing. The SEA has responsibility for assisting LEAs in this regard.

7. Opportunity for an appeal procedure to SEA for an impartial review if hearings are held at LEA level. The review officer shall make an independent decision upon completion of the review.

Requires the dissemination of information regarding parent's rights, and the steps that may be taken, should aggrieved parties wish to appeal to SEA for review of a hearing.

8. Opportunity for any party to a hearing to have counsel, to present evidence, to cross examine, to receive a written verbatim record, and a written finding of fact. The decision is also to be transmitted to the state advisory committee.

Legal proceedings may consume additional time and expenditure of funds in a local district. More staff may be needed at the time of a hearing.

9. Opportunity for any party to bring civil action in any state or district court of the United States regarding complaint, if party is aggrieved by results of hearing. The

court shall receive records and hear additional evidence.

10. Opportunity for the child to remain in his current educational program during all hearings and court actions, unless parents and school otherwise agree.

Child must not be denied services because of legal proceedings.

11. District courts of the United States shall have jurisdiction of actions in these cases.

X. Withholding and Judicial Review

Implications for Local School Districts

1. Whenever the Commissioner has found SEAs or LEAs to be in noncompliance, and has provided adequate notice and an opportunity for a hearing, he shall withhold further payments to the state and may, in addition, withhold payments to states for vocational education funds.

2. The Commissioner may withhold funds for portions of the program not in compliance. Or states may withhold funds from LEAs not in compliance. The Commissioner or the SEA shall continue to withhold funds until there is satisfaction that a failure to comply no longer exists.

LEAs are monitored for compliance by SEAs. Failure to comply may result in withholding of funds.

3. SEAs must bring the Commissioner's action to the attention of the general public.

In like manner, LEAs must bring the SEA's action to withhold LEA funds, to the attention of the public.

4. If a state is dissatisfied with the Commissioner's action regarding the state plan, the state may file with the U.S. Court of Appeals for a petition to review the action.

5. Final judgment of the court is subject to review by the Supreme Court.

XI.   Administration of PL 94-142 by the U.S. Commissioner of Education:

The Commissioner shall:

1.   Furnish technical assistance necessary, directly or by grant or contract, to states, for execution of provisions under the Act.

2.   Assure that each state shall, within one year after enactment of PL 94-142, provide certification of the exact number of children receiving special education and related services.

3.   Require a uniform financial report to be utilized by SEAs in submitting their annual state plans.

4.   Amend or revoke such rules or regulations as necessary, by January 1, 1977.

5.   Provide assurance that the secretary to the Commissioner shall take action to assure protection of confidentiality of records collected or maintained by the Commissioner.

XII.   Evaluation of PL 94-142 by Commissioner

1.   The Commissioner shall evaluate the impact and effectiveness of the program.

2.   The Commissioner shall conduct directly, or by grant or contract studies, those investigations and evaluations that are necessary to insure effective implementation of the Act.

Implications for Local School Districts

Federal assistance given to SEAs for implementation.

Your district must cooperate in child find and child count activities.

Technical assistance to SEAs may be necessary.

The rules and regulations under PL 94-142 were published in the Federal Register dated August 23, 1977. A modified procedure for determining the eligibility of learning disabled students was published in a later Federal Register, dated December 29, 1977.

Confidentiality is assured at all levels.

Implications for Local School Districts

The U. S. Commissioner of Education assumes over-all evaluation responsibility of PL 94-142.

3. The Commissioner shall provide to Congress updated programmatic information from SEAs and LEAs. Information shall include:

- Number of handicapped children in each state, within each disability, who require special education.

  LEA cooperation to SEA, and SEA cooperation and assistance to federal evaluation efforts, are necessary.

- Number of handicapped children receiving services, and number of handicapped children not receiving services.
- Number of handicapped children in regular education, and number of handicapped children in separate facilities or classes.

  LEA cooperation in child census, child find, and child identification.

- Number of handicapped children in public or private institutions receiving services, and number of handicapped children in such institutions not receiving services.
- Amount of federal, state, and local expenditures in each state, available for special education and related services.

  Your LEA must report funds available for special education services.

- Number of personnel, by disability category, employed in the education of handicapped children, plus number needed to carry out policy established by the Act.

4. Evaluation of program effectiveness, and validation of the testing and evaluation methods.

LEAs must cooperate with SEA to furnish information to the Commissioner. This includes personnel information and program evaluation methods.

XIII. Incentive Grants

Commissioner shall make a grant to each state which, in addition to the other requirements of the act,

Implications for Local School Districts

Additional authorized dollars; however, no appropriations have been set. An approved application

provides services to handicapped
children aged 3-5, at $300 per child.

will be needed.

XIV. Payments Under PL 94-142

**Implications for Local School
Districts**

Commissioner shall make payments
to states in amounts to which they
are entitled. Payments may be made
in advance, or by reimbursement in
installments, as the Commissioner
determines necessary.

Payment schedule to the 50 states is
Commissioner's decision.

Appendix B

A Helpful Selection of Sample Forms*

Here are some forms, many of which are to be used for parental information of one kind or another. The way you adapt them for your district's use depends on the people you're communicating with. We have made no attempt to word these forms, or the ones given earlier in this book, so that they serve all your patrons. That might be an impossible task. For the most part, the samples we have here are suitable for a sizeable cross section of our country's middle class. But because some parents don't read at the level of these forms, you may want to rework them into a more easily read style. If the forms you send out are consistently disregarded or misinterpreted, a change in style might be what is needed. Be wary of anything slangy, or bordering on "talking down" to parents.

And don't forget the non-English group. For a community where a number of families speaks a foreign language in the home — for example, Spanish — it may be worthwhile to have the commonly used forms translated for future use.

---

*Some of the forms and procedural guidelines in this book have been adapted from programs established in various school districts. While no one agency is responsible for any one form, readers will find that portions of the procedures are sufficiently flexible so as to simplify adjustment to fit a particular situation.

Sample 1
SCREENING FORM
(Can also be titled a Request for Evaluation form)

DATE _____

STUDENT _____ BD _____ GRADE _____

SCHOOL _____ TEACHER _____

STUDENT'S ADDRESS _____

HOME LOCATION _____

PARENT OR GUARDIAN'S NAME _____ PHONE _____

_____

Specific Reason for Referral _____

_____

Describe specific skills (academic, social, etc.) student needs to function in your classroom: _____

_____

Describe steps taken to provide for individual's needs in the classroom: _____

_____

_____

_____

Results of above _____

_____

Parent Contacts _____

Parent Concerns _____

_____

HEALTH INFORMATION:

Vision _____ Hearing _____ General Health _____

General Comments _____

TEST INFORMATION:

    Most recent achievement test _____Date _____

    Other tests (name and date) _____

Agencies involved with individual _____

ADMINISTRATOR'S COMMENTS:

Referral From:

    Teacher _____   Principal _____

    Parent _____   Nurse _____

    Agency _____

    Other _____

_____

Teacher's Signature   Date

_____

Principal's Signature   Date

Sample 2
PRIOR NOTICE TO PARENTS CONCERNING INTENT TO REFER FOR EVALUATION
(Can be sent out after screening process)

Date _____

Dear _____

There is a possibility that your child, _____, BD _____, may not be receiving the full benefit of the schooling available to him. A review of your child's progress indicates that additional information may help us better evaluate his educational needs and plan the most appropriate educational program.

Reasons for Concern: _____

_____

_____

Attempts to Resolve Concerns (within your child's current educational program):

_____

_____

_____

As a result of the above concern(s), we feel it is necessary to collect additional educational information. Qualified school personnel are currently identifying tests and evaluation procedures that are appropriate for your child. A letter will be sent to you in the near future describing intended evaluation procedures and asking your permission prior to any testing.

In an effort to keep you fully informed as to your rights concerning educational evaluation and placements, it is important that you understand you have the right to:

1. Review all records related to your child's referral for evaluation,
2. Review all procedures and instruments to be used in the evaluation,
3. Refuse to permit evaluation(s) or a change in your child's educational placement,
4. Be fully informed of the results of evaluation,
5. Obtain an independent evaluation for your child from a public or private agency,
6. Request an impartial due process hearing, and
7. Permit or deny disclosure of your child's school records to anyone other than school personnel.

If, as a result of our evaluation, your child's school placement needs further consideration, you will be notified and invited to a meeting to help plan your child's educational program. We will not change your child's school placement without your written permission.

If you would like to request a parent conference to discuss the progress of your child or explain any part of this notice, please call _____,

at _____. (phone number).

Sincerely,

_____
Principal

Sample 3
PARENT CONSENT FORM
FOR DIAGNOSTIC TESTING
(Initial Evaluation)

Dear _____:

In a prior communication (personal interview or mail), you have been informed of the school's concern for your child's educational progress and the need to gather further information so that the best possible program can be planned. The law requires that you approve of any individual testing or other individual evaluation of your child before we may proceed. Please read the attached explanation of the tests, and of your rights,* and sign as indicated below. Your cooperation is appreciated.

The evaluation procedures to be used in each of the following areas are:

Intelligence: (explain)

Communication: (explain)

Physical: (explain)

Behavior: (explain)

Academic: (explain)

Other: (explain)

Date _____

I have been informed of the referral of my child, _____ , BD _____ , for individual testing or other evaluation procedures indicated above. I have received a copy of "Explanation of Procedural Safeguards and Due Process" and understand my rights.

☐ Permission is given to conduct the evaluation as described.

☐ I request a conference to discuss the referral of my child.

☐ I request a conference to discuss my rights as outlined on the attached notice.

_____

Parent's signature

_____

Date

PLEASE READ AND KEEP THE ATTACHED PAGES. RETURN THIS PAGE TO:

_____

Administrator's Name

_____

Address

*A copy of these rights is in Chapter 11, Figure 11-7. It should be enclosed with this form letter.

Sample 4
ASSESSMENT (#1)

TO: Examining Physician
FROM: Special Education Administrator
REGARDING: Student _____ BD _____
                Address _____
                School _____

In order to develop an appropriate educational plan for the above named student, it is necessary that he/she receive a physical examination. The purpose of the examination is to determine (1) whether there are any physical factors which might contribute to educational problems, (2) whether treatment is needed prior to the offering of education in a special instructional program, and (3) whether any other specialized type of examination is indicated.

Specific psychological and educational information will be furnished with written parental permission.

1. Summary of medical examination for the above named child (to include hearing and vision).

    _____

    _____

    _____

2. Is the child in need of medical care?   Yes _____ No _____
    If medical care is needed, is it likely to improve scholastic ability if treatment is provided?   Yes _____ No _____

3. Is any other specialized type of medical examination indicated before developing an individual education plan for this student?   Yes _____ No _____
    If answer is "yes," to whom will you refer the child? _____

    _____

4. Is there any additional information you wish to include? _____

    _____

(THE MEDICAL REPORT IS TO BE RETURNED TO
ADMINISTRATOR OF SPECIAL EDUCATION)

Name _____Address _____

_____

Physician's Signature   Date

_____

Address

Sample 5
ASSESSMENT (#2)

Evaluation Summary for Certification of Specific Learning Disabilities

Student's Name: _____ BD _____ School: _____

Grade: _____

1. **HEALTH INFORMATION:**

   R   L   : R   L

   Vision: wo: _____ w: _____

   R   L   R   L

   Hearing: _____

   General Health: _____

2. **ABILITY:** It is estimated that this student is of _____ intellectual ability on the basis of (check one or more):

   ☐ our judgment

   ☐ test results: _____ :

   ☐ other: _____ .

3. **ACHIEVEMENT:** He/she is not achieving commensurate with his/her age and grade level as documented by (list tests and scores):

   _____
   _____
   _____

4. **CLASS OBSERVATION:** _____ has observed this student in the regular classroom, and the following is a summary of this observation:

5. **SEVERE DISCREPANCY STATEMENT:** On the basis of the above summarized information, there is a severe discrepancy between this student's achievement and intellectual ability in the following area(s):

   ☐ oral expression   ☐ reading comprehension
   ☐ listening comprehension   ☐ mathematics calculation
   ☐ written expression   ☐ mathematics reasoning
   ☐ basic reading

6. **IMPACT STATEMENT:** Summary of the effects of environmental, cultural, and/or economic disadvantage upon this student's achievement.

Sample 5 (Continued)

7. MEDICAL: Has there been a recent medical examination of this student?

————Yes ————No

a. If yes, indicate educationally relevant medical findings: _____
_____
_____

b. If no, please check the appropriate box below:

☐ We recommend that the School District waive the medical examination generally required in determining eligibility of handicapped children for special education with the understanding that an examination will be requested if this student fails to make reasonable progress after a period of special education help.

☐ We recommend that this student receive a medical examination for the following reason(s): _____
_____
_____

8. RECOMMENDATIONS — OBJECTIVES:

_____
_____
_____
_____
_____

The content of this report accurately reflects our conclusions.

DATE: _____ **STUDY TEAM SIGNATURES:**

Principal: _____ Regular Class Teacher: _____

Diagnostician: _____

Others: _____

_____

Sample 6
ASSESSMENT (#3)

(Can be used as part of mental retardation assessment)

Student _____ BD _____ School _____ Grade _____

PSYCHOLOGICAL SERVICES	Date Given	Examiner
WISC or Binet	_____	_____
Bender	_____	_____
Draw-a-Person	_____	_____
Other _____	_____	_____

ASSESSMENT		
Peabody Individual Achievement Test	_____	_____
Spraings Perceptual Analysis — Test B	_____	_____
Durrell Visual Memory	_____	_____
Wepman Auditory Discrimination I and II . . .	_____	_____
Auditory-Verbal Learning Test (E. M. Taylor) .	_____	_____
Listening Comprehension (Spache)	_____	_____
Oral Rated Inventory	_____	_____
Written Rated Inventory	_____	_____
Oral Commissions Test (Detroit)	_____	_____
Time Relationships — Past, Present, Future . .	_____	_____
Parts of the Body	_____	_____
Right-Left Awareness (Piaget)	_____	_____
Motor-Free Visual Perception Test (MVPT) . .	_____	_____
Key Math	_____	_____
Other _____	_____	_____
_____	_____	_____
_____	_____	_____
_____	_____	_____
_____	_____	_____
_____	_____	_____

Sample 7
ASSESSMENT (#4)

(Can be used in some cases when parents are interviewed.
The interviewer should elicit the information.)

Does your child _____, BD _____, have difficulty in:

   Seeing? _____ . _____

                 (describe)

   Hearing? _____ . _____

   Standing? _____ . _____

   Walking? _____ . _____

Is your child often ill? _____ . _____

Does he have heart trouble? _____ . _____

Does he have seizures? _____ . _____

Does he have any other physical disabilities or defects? _____ . _____

_____

Toileting

   Bowels controlled _____

   Bladder control: In daytime _____ At night _____

Feeding

   _____ Feeds self alone   _____ Eats most foods

   _____ With some help   _____ Eats few foods

   _____ No self-feeding   _____ Eats solid foods

Communication

How does he let you know his wants?

   _____ Talks   _____ Makes facial expressions

   _____ Makes sounds   _____ Gestures

Speech

   _____ Understandable   _____ Uses sentences

   _____ Uses words   _____ Can speak but seldom does

Behavior Characteristics

   _____ excitable   _____ is attentive

   _____ inactive   _____ has temper tantrums

   _____ overactive   _____ cares for own and other's belongings

   _____ willing to follow requests   _____ is aware of danger

   _____ plays with other children   _____ has few interests

   _____ teases others   _____ has unusual interests

   _____ hits or hurts others   _____ prolonged crying or giggling

   _____ has no chance to play with children   _____ is not apparently interested in people

   _____ is afraid of (list fears)   _____ is interested in only one or two people

   _____

   _____

   _____

Sample 7 (continued)

What do you feel your child needs now?

_____ to learn to read

_____ to learn colors

_____ to learn to do basic arithmetic

_____ to learn to write

_____ to learn to talk

_____ to improve his speech

_____ to learn to concentrate

_____ to learn better muscular control

_____ to acquire manual skills

_____ to become more independent

_____ to learn how to go about community alone

_____ to learn simple work that he can do independently at home

_____ to become more relaxed

_____ to calm down

_____ to have more fun

_____ help in adjusting to other children

_____ a chance to be with other children regularly

_____ to become more cooperative

_____ toilet training

_____ to learn to feed self

_____ to learn to dress self

Other Comments:

Sample 8
ASSESSMENT (#5)

ASSESSMENT DATA SUMMARY SHEET

Name: _____ BD: _____ School: _____ Grade: _____ Date: _____

Assessment Area Codes:

A.A. — Academic Achievement

S.A. — Social Adaption

V. — Prevocational & Vocational

P.S. — Psychomotor Skills

S.H.S. — Self-Help Skills

Date of Test	Evaluation Area/Method and Examiner	Results and Test Behavior	Educational Implications

Sample 9
ASSESSMENT (#6)

ELIGIBILITY CONFERENCE REPORT
(A meeting to evaluate child's eligibility
for special education.)

Eligibility Conference Date: _____

Child's Name: _____ BD _____

Address: _____ Parent: _____

School: _____ Category of Handicapping Condition: _____

Criteria for Eligibility	Assessments and Evaluations Used to Meet Criteria	Name and Title of Evaluator	Date of Evaluation

Members of Evaluation Committee

Name	Position
Name	Position
Name	Position

The above named child is certified handicapped and eligible for special education services according to state statutes and rules. Written parent permission must be obtained before placement.

Signed _____ Date _____
                    Administrator of Special Education

The above named child is not eligible for special education services because _____

_____

Signed _____ Date _____
                    Administrator of Special Education

Sample 10
ASSESSMENT (#7)

SHARING THE ASSESSMENT WITH PARENTS.
- (Can be combined with an IEP meeting.
Also, parent permission Form-for-Placement (Sample 11),
can be signed at this meeting.)

Date _____

Dear _____:

In order for the evaluation program to be effective for each child, it is important that school personnel and parents work together as a team.

As you know, we have been completing an educational assessment of your child _____ _____ BD _____ We would like to meet with you to share information from the completed assessments. At this meeting you will have the opportunity to assist in the development of educational objectives for your child, along with the other team members. The results of this meeting will be the development of the most appropriate education program for your child.

The meeting will be on _____ at _____ in _____
　　　　　　　　　　　　　　　(date)　　　　　　　　　　　　(time)

_____
　　　　(location)

If you are unable to attend this meeting, please contact us at _____
　　　　　　　　　　　　　　　　　　　　　　　　　　　　　(phone)

as soon as possible in order to plan a time which is mutually convenient.

It is possible that as a result of this meeting your child's educational placement may change. No change, however, will be authorized without your permission. In order to keep you fully informed and involved concerning decisions about your child, federal and state rules and regulations require that parents be informed of the following whenever the school district proposes to initiate or change the identification, evaluation or placement of a student:

1. You have the right to review all your child's school records.
2. You have the right to review all tests and evaluation procedures.
3. You have the right to refuse to permit evaluations or changes in your child's educational placement.
4. You have the right to be fully informed of the results of evaluations of your child.
5. You have the right to obtain an independent evaluation at public expense.
6. You have the right to request an impartial due process hearing.
7. You have the right to give prior consent or deny the disclosure of your child's school records to anyone other than education personnel.

　　　　　　　　　　　Sincerely,

_____
Administrator of Special Education

_____
Address

Sample 11

PARENT CONSENT FORM-FOR-PLACEMENT

(Completed at time of Assessment-Review and Education-Planning (IEP) Meeting if parent is present. Send with Sample 12, by registered mail, if parent is not present).

Date _____

I, as parent or guardian, hereby
☐ give my consent,
☐ do not give my consent,
for the placement of _____, BD _____
in the special education program.

Exceptionality Areas:

_____Speech Handicapped (Communication Disorders)

_____Mentally Retarded

_____Learning Disabilities

_____Emotionally Disturbed

_____Visually Impaired

_____Physically Handicapped

_____Hearing Impaired

Additional Notations: _____

_____

_____

(Parent or Guardian) Signature

_____

(Administrator of Special Education) Signature

_____

Address

Sample 12

LETTER TO PARENT WHO DID NOT ATTEND THE ASSESSMENT-REVIEW AND EDUCATION-PLANNING (IEP) MEETING.

(Requests parents to sign Parent Consent Form-for-Placement (Sample 11), which should be enclosed. The "meeting report" mentioned in the letter is a copy of the child's IEP, Sample 13.)

Date _____

Dear _____:

A meeting to which you were invited, but did not attend, met on _____ to consider an appropriate educational program plan for your child, _____ _____, BD _____ A copy of the meeting report is enclosed.*

You will note that the report includes recommendations for placement which were made after consideration of all the available information.

If you agree with the recommendations, please sign the enclosed consent form and return it in the envelope provided. If you disagree, there is a statement of parental rights and procedures indicating next steps to follow.

Sincerely,

Encls.

_____

Administrator of Special Education

_____

Address

_____

*With this letter you enclose Samples 11 and 13.

Sample 12 (continued)

STATEMENT OF PARENTAL RIGHTS AND PROCEDURES
CONCERNING PLACEMENT

The following procedures safeguard your rights in planning for the future education of your child:

1. You may sign the enclosed parent consent form which permits your child to be placed in the special education program appropriate to his/her needs.

2. You may choose not to sign the enclosed form and may request an additional conference to get further information.

3. You may desire an independent medical, psychological, and educational evaluation of your child by an agency other than that provided by this school system. Our school office will assist you in acquiring this independent evaluation.

4. If you do not agree with the placement recommendation for your child, and an impasse has been reached between you and the local school district, you may refuse to sign the consent form and may request a hearing before an independent Hearing Officer. If such a hearing is desired, please make your request in writing within twenty (20) days of the date of this letter, to the Superintendent of _____ at this office. You may use the attached form for this request.
    (Local School District)

_____   _____
Administrator of Special Education   Superintendent (Local School District)

                                        _____
                                        (Address)

Sample 12 (continued)

REQUEST FOR DUE PROCESS HEARING

I (We), _____, have reviewed the proposed instructional plan for my (our) child, _____ BD _____, and I (we) wish to appeal for a further review of the recommended program. I (we) understand that my (our) child will remain in the present educational placement until such time as there is a decision, following the due process hearing, or until a proposed educational placement is accepted by the parties.

Signed _____

Mailing Address _____

_____

Phone _____

1. It is important for you to understand the following. During the hearing procedures the parent has the right:
   - To be represented by legal counsel.
   - To bring witnesses.
   - To request certain school personnel to be present.
   - To cross examine.
   - To obtain an independent evaluation.
   - To request a "closed" hearing if desired.
   - To examine and reproduce all school records.
   - To verbatim record of the hearing, if requested.
   - To determine if the child shall attend the hearing. Wherever appropriate, a child 18 years or older makes this decision.

2. The burden of proof as to the adequacy and appropriateness of the proposed course of action shall be upon the local education agency.

3. At all stages of the hearing, interpretation for the deaf and interpreters in the primary language of the home (when other than English) shall be provided at public expense.

Sample 13

INDIVIDUALIZED EDUCATION PROGRAM WRITE-UP

Student's Name _____ BD _____

School and
School District _____ Date of meeting: _____

Pre-set date for review _____

_____

Pre-set date for next full evaluation _____

Current Placement _____	Persons Present	Relationship to child
Eligibility certified for Special Education _____ date	_____	_____
Period of current individualized education program	_____	_____
	_____	_____
_____ to _____ (dates)	_____	_____
	_____	_____

A. Curriculum areas requiring special education and related services (include physical education)	Present Level(s) of Performance	Annual Goals	Short Term Objectives	Time for Attainment	Objectives Attained (Dates)
Area 1 Ex. Math					
Area 2 Ex. Reading					

B. Special education and related services	Personnel Responsible (Name and Position)	Date Services Begin	Duration
Curriculum Area 1 (as in item A above) Ex. Math			
Curriculum Area 2 (as in item A above) Ex. Reading			

Sample 13 (continued)

C. Short term objectives (as in item A above)	Objective Criteria	Evaluation Procedures	Outcome Data

D. Extent to which the child will participate in regular education program placement.

E. Other placement and educational alternatives considered, and reasons for acceptance or rejection.

Sample 14

REQUEST FOR RELEASE OF
CONFIDENTIAL INFORMATION

Date _____

To Whom It May Concern:
          I hereby authorize _____
to give any or all information contained in the school record of:

          Student's Name _____
          Birthdate _____
          Father's Name _____
          Mother's Name _____
To: Name of Requesting Person _____
          Agency or School _____
          Address _____
          City and State _____

_____   _____
Date   Signature of Parent, Legal Guardian, or Student
                         if appropriate and of legal age

                         _____
                         Witness (Name and School Position)

Sample 15

A SAMPLE POLICY STATEMENT PERTAINING TO A FREE APPROPRIATE EDUCATION FOR ALL HANDICAPPED CHILDREN

It is the intent of School District _____ to develop, refine, and implement programs that assure that all handicapped children within the jurisdiction of the School District have available to them a free appropriate public education which emphasizes special education and related services designed to meet their unique needs. The district seeks to assure that handicapped children's rights and their parents' rights are protected, and that confidentiality of personally identifiable material is in operation at all times. The free appropriate public education provided for handicapped children will meet the standards of the State Educational Agency and will be in conformity with the individualized education program required by Public Law 94-142.

The _____ School Board directs the school district administration to (1) provide and disseminate all information and directives that are necessary to carry out the above intent, (2) see that the directives are implemented, and (3) provide schedules and measurement devices for determining whether the Board's intent, as described in the above paragraph, is being carried out.

Adopted by the _____ School District Board of Directors on _____

Index